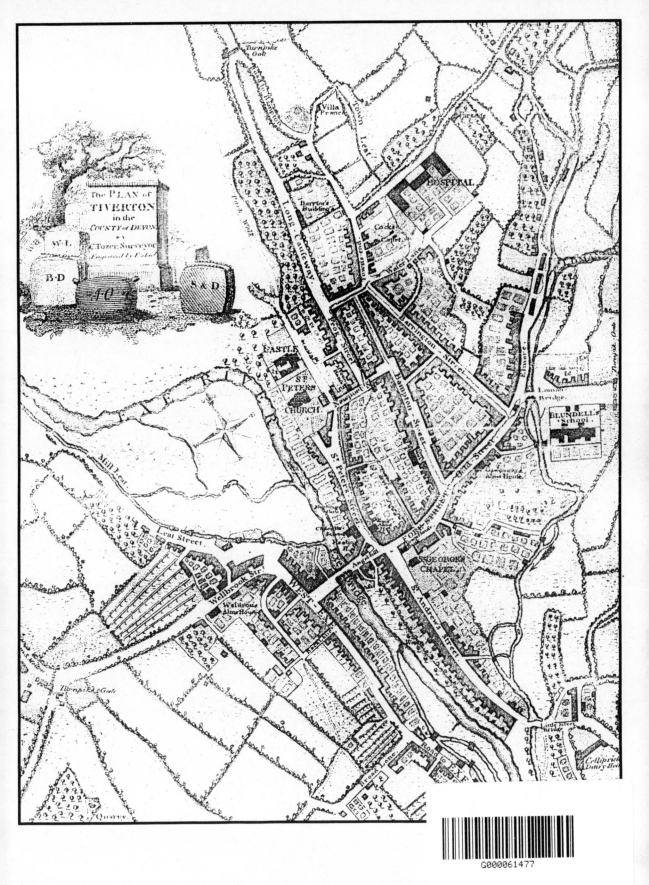

The PLAN of
TIVERTON
in the
COUNTY of DEVON
BY
C. Tozer, Surveyor.
Engraved by Esher.

TIVERTON
and the
EXE VALLEY

A Pictorial History

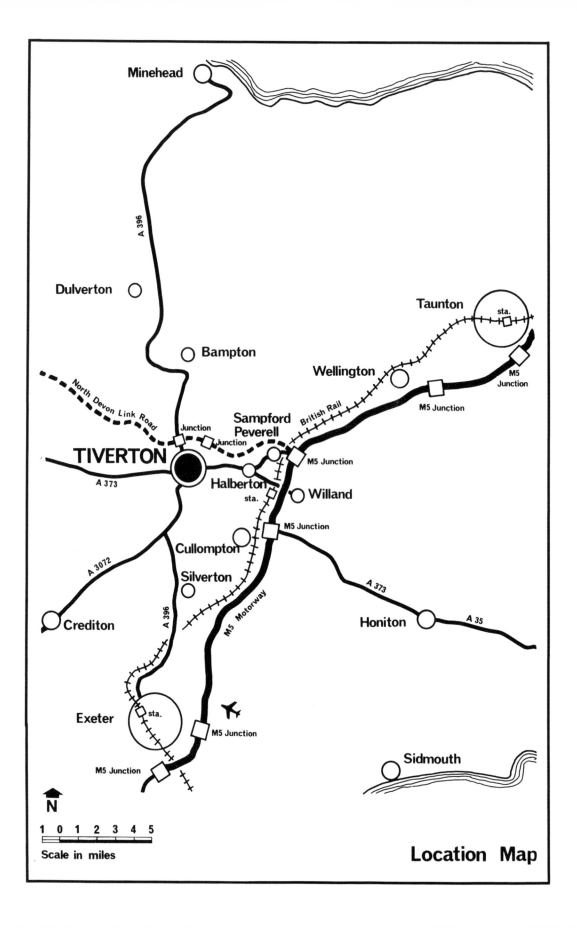

Minehead

A 396

Dulverton

Bampton

Taunton sta.

Wellington

M5 Junction

North Devon Link Road

British Rail

M5 Junction

Junction

Sampford Peverell

Junction

TIVERTON

A 373

Halberton sta.

M5 Junction

Willand

M5 Junction

Cullompton

A 3072

Silverton

M5 Motorway

A 373

Honiton

A 35

Crediton

A 396

Exeter sta.

M5 Junction

M5 Junction

Sidmouth

N

1 0 1 2 3 4 5

Scale in miles

Location Map

TIVERTON
and the
EXE VALLEY
A Pictorial History

Mary de la Mahotière

Phillimore

1990

Published by
PHILLIMORE & CO. LTD.
Shopwyke Hall, Chichester, Sussex

ISBN 0 85033 738 0

Printed and bound in Great Britain by
BIDDLES LTD.
Guildford, Surrey

The West Wind

It's a warm wind, the west wind, full of birds' cries;
I never hear the west wind but tears are in my eyes
For it comes from the west lands, the old brown hills,
And April's in the west wind, and daffodils.

John Masefield

List of Illustrations

Frontispiece: location map of Tiverton

Acknowledgements

These photographs appear by kind permission of the following: Tiverton Castle (Angus and Alison Gordon), 6, 7, 33; Bickleigh Castle (Noel and Norma Boxall), 8, 9, 11, 44; Knightshayes (David Crooks), 70, 71, 73; Joyce, Lady Amory, 162, 164; Withleigh (J. Gibson), 76; Blundell's School (Brian Jenkins), 97-102, 137, 138; Fursdon House (David Fursdon), 34b; Norman Young, 37, 38; W. Seymour, 135, 161; A.J.N. Carpenter, 168; Lena Knight, 82; Graham Stirling, 2, 34a; Tidcombe Hall, 32; Brian Butler, 125; F. Williams, 126, 127, 129, 141; Heathcoat Factory (John Gibson), 52-57, 131, 132, 136, 171, 172; Tiverton Civic Society (John Keene), 20, 26, 36, 47; Tiverton Museum (Alan Voce), 4, 31, 41, 51, 75, 90, 94, 95, 114-18, 128, 149, 151, 154-7, 159, 160, 165-7, 174; Robert Wilson, 45, 46; *White Horse Inn*, 35; Roger Jeanes, 91, 96; Bob Butler, 3; Tom Penny, 19b; West Country Tourist Board, 148. Other photographs supplied by the author, some from material kindly lent by Victor Broomfield, Leslie Slade and Bruce Hoare. Reproduction of map of Tiverton Hundred, Anne Welsford (*A Church and Its People*); Map of Grand Western Canal, Mid Devon County Council.

The Town of Two Fords

The early history of Tiverton was dictated by two rivers, the Exe (*Isca*) and the Lowman, which meet at Collipriest, just south of the town. It was from the fords across these rivers that the name Tiverton, Twi-ford town, derived.

The Exe was a formidable obstacle; this can be a dangerous and treacherous river. It rises high up on a desolate plateau on Exmoor. Once free of the moor, it hurries on to Dulverton, soon joined by the Barle, the Batherm and a whole army of anonymous streams draining off the steep coombes. By the time it reaches Tiverton, it has picked up speed; in spate, it rushes at the town, wielding a battering ram of fallen trees. A few hundred yards to the east is the Lowman, a short, deceptively innocent-looking and unpredictable river which can bring havoc to that side of town.

The way to Cullompton, Exeter and the east lay across these two rivers, then upwards over the steep hills above them; valley bottoms were impassable. Intrepid men, thousands of years before Alfred, using primitive axes (local finds from Withleigh, Ash Thomas and Worth can be seen at the Museum) hacked a way through the dark and threatening forests to the banks of the Exe. Later, Iron Age invaders established themselves in hill-top forts like the great Hembury Fort, near Honiton, and, in the Exe valley, Cadbury Castle near Thorverton, Huntsham Castle near Bampton, and Cranmore Castle at Tiverton. Cranmore Castle on Skrinkhills overlooks the confluence of the Exe and Lowman and commands a wide view of the rivers and the town. Few traces remain of the fortifications on the hill-top, later occupied by the *Dumnonii*, a tribe whose territory covered most of Devon and Cornwall with headquarters at Exeter (*Isca Dumnoniorum*).

The settlement around the two river crossings was for centuries thought to have been ignored by the Romans but excavations on the hill at Bolham, near Knightshayes, recently uncovered a Roman fort there, occupied *c*.A.D. 50 by some 500 men of the Augusta II Legion. A model was presented to the Museum in 1989.

By the time of Alfred, the settlement had become a royal manor. In his will *c*.899 he left to his younger son, Ethelweard, 'the land at Collumpton and at Twyfyrde'. When, in the early 10th century, local government was organised into hundreds, Tiverton was the obvious choice to become the focal point for the local gathering (moot) where envoys from local manors and nearby villages or tythings would meet to hear royal proclamations and to consider, with the portreeve, matters of taxation, crime and land ownership. The boundary of the hundred roughly coincides with the later confines of the parish. Today, the Bailiff of the Hundred, carrying his ancient staff of office, officiates only at the seven-yearly Perambulation of the Leat (gifted to Tiverton in 1250). Later, all the rich farmlands of the royal manor were divided up; one isolated pocket still remains in the ownership of the monarch's son – Bradninch, part of the Duchy of Cornwall.

Norman Conquest

In 1066, the royal manor of Tiverton belonged to Gytha, Danish-born widow of Earl Godwin. Their daughter, Edith, had married the saintly Edward the Confessor. When he

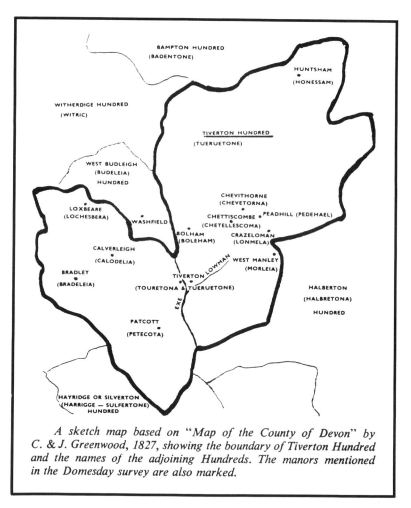

A sketch map based on "Map of the County of Devon" by C. & J. Greenwood, 1827, showing the boundary of Tiverton Hundred and the names of the adjoining Hundreds. The manors mentioned in the Domesday survey are also marked.

died without an heir in January 1066, Gytha's son, Harold, was chosen by the witan (parliament) to succeed him. Rightly or wrongly, William of Normandy laid claim to the throne and, having defeated Harold at the battle of Hastings, proceeded to subdue the kingdom of Wessex. Loyal supporters of Gytha, hearing that Exeter had closed its gates against William's advancing army, made their way over the hills to lend support but Exeter was forced to surrender within days. Gytha escaped across the Channel. Tiverton was now at the mercy of the Conqueror.

The assessment in Domesday, 1086, of Tovretone, a manor held by Gytha, Mother of Harold, reads 'Before 1066 it paid tax for 3½ hides'. A hide was approximately 120 acres. 'Land for 36 ploughs. The King has 1½ hides in lordship. 35 villagers, 24 smallholders and 19 slaves with 30 ploughs and 2 hides. 3 pigmen who pay 10 pigs. 2 mills which pay 66d. Meadow, 14 acres; common pasture, 40 acres; woodland, 4 furlongs; [...]' – word omitted, perhaps 'underwood' or, more probably, a second 'stretch of woodland' – '1 league in length and 6½ furlongs in width. 28 sheep. Value £18 weighed and assayed.'

Tiverton was, then, a small but prosperous town. Domesday shows in detail how each and every one of Gytha's hapless supporters was supplanted by the Norman soldiers, prelates or courtiers whom William rewarded with the spoils of war.

When William's younger son, Henry I, came to the throne in 1100, he was plagued by nightmares that the two great powers, the lords and the church, would be joined by the commoners and rise against him. He commanded Richard de Redvers, his 'faithful and beloved Councillor', to build a castle at Tiverton, creating him Earl of Devon. On the high bluff some 100 ft. above the Exe, he built the motte and bailey castle which commanded the river crossing and was almost impregnable. Curtain walls surrounded an acre of land and towers rose at each corner; the Exe protected its western flank, on the other three sides were moats. The main entrance was, as today, through the fortified eastern gateway. The defensive outworks, still known as 'The Works', stretched out to Redgate and to Castle Street (formerly known as Frog Street from the amphibious residents in the moats and in the Leat which bisects the street). Here was the tilting-yard where the castle horsemen and retainers could practise their skill, long remembered as the old 'Hit-or-Miss Court', later corrupted to 'Hippopotamus Court' and today Castle Place.

Already, the Church of St Peter, sharing the same escarpment as the castle, had been built, probably to replace a humble Saxon wooden chapel on the same site. Consecrated by Leofric, first Bishop of Exeter, in 1073, it was easily accessible from the castle. Only the Norman doorway, with its typical zigzag carving around an arch, has survived subsequent rebuilding. Richard de Redvers' son, Baldwin, who succeeded his father in 1130, was responsible for the unique arrangement by which the parish of Tiverton was administered in four portions, Clare, Pitt, Tidcombe and Prior, right up to 1886 when Bishop Temple rationalised the position. Baldwin gave the whole church of Tiverton 'with all its appurtenances' to the Cluniac monastery of St James in Exeter. Bitter disputes followed. The monks were accused of being too concerned with small matters such as what boots and attire priests should wear on horseback and of seriously neglecting the church at Tiverton and its huge parish. By 1259, however, the priory controlled only one portion and de Redvers was patron of Clare, Pitt and Tidcombe.

In an age when religion ruled men's lives, this greatly increased the power of the castle. Throughout these early centuries, Tiverton dwelt in the shadow of the castle and under the overlordship of the two great families who lived there, the de Redvers and, later, the Courtenays. Their power was absolute. Typical was Isabella de Fortibus, Countess of Devon in her own right. This formidable lady had 'Countess Wear' constructed across the river below Exeter, so bringing water to her mills and tolls from the port of Topsham to her coffers, but depriving Exeter of access to the port. Exeter had to build its ship canal.

It was Isabella (or possibly her mother, Amicia), however, who gave c.1250, in perpetuity, a 'stream of pure water' rising some five miles north, on Norwood Common, to the people of Tiverton – it was also very handy for the castle! It runs through Chettiscombe to reach Tiverton at 'World's End', so called because it is on the northernmost perimeter of the town where the road leads on to Bampton and the great moors beyond. It flows on through Castle Street and the Market to Coggan's Well. Here, every seven years, most recently in 1989, the Perambulation of the Leat or 'water-bailing' is declared by the Mayor with great ceremony. Then the procession sets off, the Water Bailiff, the Pioneers armed with axes to clear obstructions, and the 'withy boys' to beat the bounds with willow wands. Isabella also gave 150 acres of land at Elmore to the poor, with rights of quarrying there.

The de Redvers line died out in 1293 and the royal manor passed to a kinsman, Hugh de Courtenay. The Courtenays had come to England in 1151 with Eleanor of Aquitaine, the bride of Henry II, and, after a legal dispute, Hugh was created Earl of Devon in 1335.

Religion was still paramount. The wealthier families had long had private chapels built where they could hear mass said daily – one at Tiverton Castle had been licensed in 1329. In 1400 Bishop Stafford granted a licence to Anne, Countess of Devon, 'to have Divine Service performed in the Rectory-house of Tydcombe, where she then resided'; that same year he also licensed St Catherine's chapel at Withleigh. In Tiverton itself were four chapels, including St Mary-on-Exe-Bridge, and in all there were some 22 chapels in the outlying districts,

The castle was held by the Courtenays until 1556. Although, throughout some 500 years, Tiverton had laboured under the feudal yoke, the town had basked in the reflected glory of great deeds. Hugh, the second 'Courtenay Earl' of Devon, 'attended the King into Brittany with a great following'; he was renowned for his prowess in repulsing pirates from Normandy who harassed the south coast settlements; he gave the market tolls to the poor. Edward, the third Earl, became 'Admiral of all the King's fleet, from the mouth of the Thames westwards' and, becoming blind, was known as 'the Blind and Good Earl'. Some of the Courtenays, however, were ruthless oppressors.

Wool Brings Wealth

Towards the end of the feudal dynasty of the Courtenays, Tiverton was developing an identity of its own. Isolated in the west as it was, it had the two basic requirements for success, wool and water. The manufacture of woollen cloth had been given impetus by Edward III's introduction of Flemish weavers around 1353 – the district of 'Germanie' near the Lowman is said to date from these 'immigrants'. Although the Black Death of 1348-50 did not leave Tiverton unscathed, it indirectly contributed to her prosperity; land that could not be tilled for lack of ploughmen reverted to pasture. Apart from sheep in the immediate countryside, great flocks were raised in the north of Devon and fleeces were brought over by the shipload from Wales and Ireland. They reached Tiverton by way of Bampton, where the narrow Packhorse Way can still be seen, Chettiscombe, and the causeway leading past the former *Bampton Inn* to World's End.

Now, too, the involvement of the Courtenay family in the great affairs of state, in battles at home and in forays abroad, can be seen to have given Tivertonians much wider horizons than they might have had, land-locked in the Exe valley. Her merchants ventured far afield.

Most renowned of Tiverton's many cloth merchants was John Greenway (1460-1529), the first to trade in cloth, not wool, and founder of Tiverton's cloth marketing. He was not content to be a merely local producer of the new kerseys, material dyed in bright reds, blues and greens and lighter and finer than the old dark, heavy broadcloth. John fully appreciated that it was in London that profits were to be made. 'Born of mean parentage', he contrived to get together enough capital to make the journey there. Quickly he realised the need to join the Worshipful Company of the Drapers to which Edward had granted the monopoly of trading in cloth in London. In 1497 he became a member of this great City guild which gave him the freedom to trade without restriction. An advantage was that at his home base at Tiverton the manufacture of the now famous Tiverton kerseys was mainly a cottage industry, not hamstrung by the guilds which controlled the bigger towns and cities. Tiverton clothiers bought wool, distributed it to the cottage workers to comb, spin and weave, and completed the process at their own mills, where pieces were checked, bales marked with the merchant's 'wool-mark' and sent for sale locally or despatched to Exeter or London. Soon Greenway was a leading figure in the export trade; by 1482 he had had his own ship, the *Mary*, built at Dartmouth. With the *George*, *Trinity Greenway* and *Charity Greenway* trading mainly out of Topsham, he carried on a brisk export trade with

Holland, France, Ireland and Spain; he was even called 'the Spanish merchant'. His main exports were woollen cloth, hides and tin and his imports wine (mostly from Bordeaux, much from Spain) besides mixed cargoes of dyes, dried fruits, iron, linen, canvas, madder, and hops.

Greenway amassed a huge fortune. A very pious man in an age of piety, he devoted the greater part of his riches to building a splendid chantry chapel at St Peter's. Outside, afloat on realistic waves carved in stone, sails a whole proud fleet. Each ship is different but all carry stout guns and from the crow's nests javelins would be thrown. These are the armed merchantmen which ensured the freedom of trade in seas infested with privateers and foreign raiders. The arms of the Merchant Adventurers held equal pride of place in the chapel with those of the Drapers.

Greenway also built an almshouse in Gold Street for five old men; the small chapel bears a number of inscriptions bidding passers-by to remember him and his wife in their prayers. 'Have grace ye men and ever pray For the sowls of John and Jone Greenway.' Little did he know in 1517 that prayers for the dead were soon to be proscribed.

The old order was changing. The Reformation, which abolished 'Popish corruptions and innovations' in favour of a return to the early precepts of Christianity, caused endless dissensions. A dispute in 1549 over whether a Sampford Peverell baby should be baptised according to the new or old rites (Bishop Cranmer's new prayer book in English supplanting the Latin usage had been introduced on Whit Sunday 1549) led to the 'rebels', who had withdrawn to Cranmore Castle on Skrinkhills, being brutally put down by the King's army. Controversy between the 'traditionalists' and 'heretics' continued under 'Bloody' Mary but when Elizabeth came to the throne in 1558 to begin her long reign of nearly half a century, stability returned.

Benefactions to churches, chapels and for the relief of the poor were manifold. The table-tomb of John Waldron (1520-97) stands in the chancel of St Peter's. He built and endowed the almshouses in West Exe where many of the cottagers lived. His wool-mark, a wool-pack and a ship, are engraved in the stone along with many pious exhortations, among them: 'Depart thy goods whyl thou hast tyme After thy deathe, they are not thyne. God sav Queene Elizabeth.'

Prosperity seemed unending. Tiverton was described as 'the chief market for cloth that is in all the west parts of England'. In 1527, St Peter's had been the scene of a great royal ceremony, the funeral of Princess Katherine, youngest daughter of Edward IV. She had married William Courtenay (d.1511) and, as Countess of Devon, had lived alone as a widow at Tiverton Castle until her death. The lying-in-state, the palls of rich black velvet overlaid by cloth of gold, the processions of banners, the massed choristers, the solemn play and the distribution of chantry money to the poor marked the end of an era – the line of the Courtenays came to an end in 1556 and the castle was acquired in about 1590 by a wealthy merchant, Roger Giffard. The Tudor manor he built there became known as Giffard's Court. The three portions of the Church and the manorial lands, formerly in the gift of the Courtenays, were divided among several related families.

The Exe was still the keystone of the town's prosperity. There had been a bridge of sorts from the days of the earliest settlers. Enormous tree trunks with post holes, found during excavations for the present bridge, part of the flood prevention scheme of 1970, can be seen outside the Museum. Records of 1319 speak of the chapel of St Mary-on-Exe-Bridge. But floods perpetually took their toll and in 1448 Bishop Lacy promised an indulgence of 40 days in return for contributions to the rebuilding of the bridge. In 1570 a 'good stone bridge of five arches' was built across the river with money from the Exe Bridge Trust, established by Walter Tyrrel in 1563.

The Armada (1588) united men against the common threat. Tiverton traders had resented the loss of their overseas markets and farmers the requisitioning of their crops, stores and horses. These were confiscated to supply the huge army which arrived at Plymouth some months before the Armada put to sea and which needed constant victualling; but there was great rejoicing when victory was won. Nevertheless, the 16th century ended badly for Tiverton. First, the plague of 1591 wiped out one tenth of the population, and in 1598 a catastrophic fire burnt the town from end to end. A 'sillie flash of fire, blazing forth of a frying pan' in a poor thatched cottage in West Exe was fanned by a high sou'westerly into a mighty blaze. In less than half an hour, Tiverton lay in ruins; the cob-and-thatch houses were smouldering embers and some 50 people burnt alive. Amongst the victims was Eleanor, the 14-year-old daughter of a rich wool merchant, George Slee (d.1613) whose tomb stands near the altar of St Peter's. Probably in her memory, he bequeathed money for the building of the Slee almshouses, adjoining his Great House of St George, still occupied, though no longer by 'six poore Widdowes or Maidens of the Town or Parish of Tiverton'.

The 17th century opened well – it was a golden age for Tiverton. The royal appeal for 'disaster' funds was so successful that the town quickly rose from the ashes so that James I described it in a brief of 1612 as 'well built with many fair houses and having therein a very fair market-place'. On Lowman Green a splendid new school was opened in 1604, the gift of yet another vastly rich wool merchant, Peter Blundell, who amassed a fortune 'far beyond that of the richest merchant in Exeter' by buying wool in Ireland and transporting it into England and, like Greenway, making his way to London while maintaining his own manufacture in Tiverton. His will (1599) enjoined his 'righte deare and honorable friende Sir John Popham, Lord Chief Justice of England' to build the school for children 'born or for the most parte before the age of six years brought upp in the towne or parrish of Tyverton ... and if the same number be not filled upp, my will is that the wante shall be supplyed with the children of forreyners', children not native to Tiverton. In 1611, William Chilcott, a nephew of Blundell, built and endowed a 'free English school' with less academic ambitions in St Peter's Street.

No lesson, however, had been learnt from the Great Fire of 1598 and on 5 August 1612, a public holiday, there broke out at Patey's the dyer's near Exe bridge the 'Dog Fight Fire' – so called because it was a dog fight which distracted attention from the furnace. Fierce flames spread until the whole town was a 'red-flaming fury'. Tiverton burnt to ashes in that day and night; only the church and castle, the schools, almshouses and a few poor hovels at Elmore survived. Again, there was a royal appeal for funds to rebuild the town. It spoke of Tiverton's 'great trade in clothing which kept always in work 8,000 persons, men, women and children' and, once again, it was hugely successful. But this time, convinced that some better ordering of the town's affairs was needed, James I granted a royal charter in 1615 which gave Tiverton the status of a borough and provided for two justices, 12 capital burgesses and 12 assistant burgesses who were given power to send two members to Parliament.

This charter, with its restricted right of franchise, contained the seeds of the violent dissensions and riots which marred the 18th century. The unrest was also contributed to by disputes over the huge trade with Ireland that successful merchants like Blundell had built up; later, in the 19th century, even Blundell's bequest itself was to lead to bitter ill-feeling.

The Civil War and After

Tiverton was immensely proud of its new status as a borough. The mayor's pew in St Peter's was embellished around 1615 with handsome painted figures of a lion rampant bearing on his shield a rose and a unicorn whose own shield bore a thistle, an especial compliment to James VI of Scotland and I of England. But soon the religious turmoil of the Civil War soured the atmosphere. At first, Tiverton did not seem disposed to take any strong line against the Cromwell faction. However, in 1643, a troop of the King's dragoons took over the town despite the hostile demonstration of a crowd who pelted them with stones; one man, John Lock, was seized and hanged outside the *White Horse*. In July 1644, Tiverton was occupied by Essex and the main parliamentary army but was regained by the Royalists after the Parliamentary defeat at Lostwithiel. In 1645 the King held all of Devon and Cornwall, except Plymouth which was a Commonwealth stronghold under siege from the Royalists. Tiverton, one of the four Royalist garrisons in Devon, could not be left in the rear of the Roundhead army under General Fairfax as he moved to raise the siege in October. He skirted Royalist Exeter and brought his army to Tiverton where the loyal Sir Gilbert Talbot had taken charge of the castle. On Sunday 19 October, the Roundhead bombardment began at seven o'clock in the morning and a lucky shot broke the chain of the drawbridge of the outer fort, now long gone. The soldiers stormed in and the castle's life as a military stronghold was ended. During the autumn and winter of 1645 both Fairfax and Cromwell stayed in the town at times and the New Model Army used the castle as a depot. The townsfolk made off with stones and the bags of wool which had been used to protect vulnerable parts of the church and castle.

The Puritans now reigned supreme and repercussions were quick to follow. Clergymen who had taken the Cavalier's Oath or in some way offended against the new Puritan dispensation by their sermons or actions were ejected by the Triers (set up to try churchmen for 'malignancy', that is loyalty to the King). Christmas Day was now forbidden as a feast day, maypole dancing proscribed, Sundays sacrosanct. Typical was the fate of Richard Newte, Rector of Clare and Tidcombe portions, son of the first town clerk appointed under the 1615 charter. Found guilty by the Triers, he suffered unremitting persecution. Soldiers were billeted on him at Tidcombe Rectory, mobs stormed the house and, while he was away from home, drove out his wife, Thomasine, and the children, despite her brave defiance. Witness to the far-reaching change of order is the Cromwell Charter of 1655, now displayed at Tiverton Museum. This decreed that henceforth market day would no longer be held on Monday, but, as today, on Tuesday to avoid the profanation of the Sabbath by traders preparing their wares which had provoked God's wrath, manifested in the two great fires of 1598 and 1612.

Many of the changes were reversed on the death of Cromwell in 1658. In 1659 came the news that 'the Lord Monke was made General'; Monk was a trusted Westcountryman from near Barnstaple. In May 1660 he escorted Charles, who had landed at Dover, on a triumphal ride to London and the bells of St Peter's, silent for most of the past 11 years, except on Guy Fawkes's Day, the great Protestant festival of 5 November, pealed out joyously. Now it was the turn of the Puritans to feel apprehensive; benefices were restored to the clergy who had been dismissed. This was especially hard on the Rev. Theophilus Polwheile, M.A., one of those ejected. A deeply religious man of the church, but a 'non-conformist', he continued to worship with a small band of devout followers in private houses and the Steps Meeting House in St Peter's Street. The church he founded there in 1660, later the Congregational church, now the United Reform, has been one of the cornerstones of religious life in Tiverton.

The much-persecuted Richard Newte was restored to his benefices and was succeeded in 1678 by his son, John, the second in the line of scholarly and pious rectors of Tidcombe who have given their name to the great hill, leading to Cullompton, which rises above the old rectory. John had no time for Puritan kill-joys and, in the face of some opposition, had the magnificent organ in St Peter's built by Christian Schmidt, nephew of 'Father Schmidt' who had come from Germany to build the great organ in St Paul's Cathedral for Christopher Wren. St Peter's organ was dedicated on 13 September 1696.

John also saw the need for a new church in Tiverton. The great church of St Peter's was overcrowded with privately-owned pews and it was anticipated that if all 'dissenters' were forced by a new Act of Uniformity to worship there, chaos would result. In 1714 he laid the first stone of St George's, near the town hall. It is one of the foremost Georgian churches in the West Country, though at first not enough money was raised to complete it and it was used as a wool warehouse by a Tiverton merchant, Oliver Peard. The architect, John James, worked with Wren on St Paul's Cathedral; his other churches include St George's, Hanover Square, in London.

Political Awakening

Prosperity continued unabated into the 18th century and, in 1724, Daniel Defoe, travelling through the West Country, found that, after Exeter, Tiverton was 'the greatest manufacturing town in the county and of all the inland towns, next to it in wealth and in numbers of people'. Around 56 fulling mills were operating in the town at this time.

It was not to last. Competition became ever fiercer and by the middle of the century, trade was in decline. The discontented townsmen who had combined into Societies would rally and riot at will. They had two particular grievances: one that wool being brought in from Ireland had been through some of the processes which, rightly, should only have been done in Tiverton, and the other that it was unfair that the two Members of Parliament should be elected only by the Corporation and not by a more general franchise.

A third disastrous fire, in June 1731, contributed to the distress and disaffection; 300 houses were destroyed and over 2,000 people made homeless. Again a public appeal for funds for rebuilding drew generous support but, this time, an Act of Parliament (1732) was passed decreeing that in future all Tiverton houses must have roofs, not of thatch, but of tiles or slates and that ricks, stacks and dangerous trades must be relegated to the outskirts of the town. Meanwhile, social provisions had not been altogether neglected. A 'splendid' hospital (and workhouse) for 300 poor had been built in 1698; the food there was plentiful and the régime liberal by the standards of the day. In 1701, John Newte had set up a charity school at his own expense; shortly after, a girls' school was added. These were later known as the Blue Coat schools. The children were clothed and taught free of charge and provided with books, pens and paper.

Sporadic outbreaks of violence continued, culminating in 1765 in the worst public disorder Tiverton has ever seen. The basic grievance was that not only did the 1615 charter restrict the choice of the two Members of Parliament to the mayor and 24 burgesses but vacancies in the Corporation itself were filled by 'wheeler-dealing', without reference to the townspeople. The historian, Hoskins, called Tiverton 'one of the rottenest boroughs in England'.

When leading merchant, Oliver Peard, the effective 'party boss' for the last 20 years, died in December 1764, the townsfolk were adamant that his place should go to a Mr. Baring of Exeter who had recommended himself to them by promises and other inducements. The mayor saw Mr. Baring as an ambitious entrepreneur and when he refused to do the people's bidding, he was assaulted. When, finally, Baring was not elected, the townspeople went on the rampage, breaking up the mayor's house and property and the great weir on the Exe at Bolham, vital to his fulling mills. The Welsh Fusiliers were summoned. They arrested some of the rioters and marched them to Exeter gaol; the next year, Mayor Webber's house at Bolham was burnt down.

The century limped to a close with clear signs that a disgruntled town had absorbed current radical thinking and was determined no longer to be governed by a self-perpetuating hierarchy.

The Victorian Age

Tiverton was hard hit by the Napoleonic Wars. The 'Tiverton Fencibles' were mobilised and drilled at the Works; periodically, regiments of the militia were drafted into the town; press gangs arrived to 'recruit' able-bodied seamen; French prisoners on parole were billeted on the householders. The price of bread and even of potatoes soared beyond the reach of the poor.

Worse was the loss of European markets on which the wool merchants depended and this loss was aggravated by the rise of the cotton industry. The new wool factory, which it was hoped would replace the uneconomic cottage industry, closed in 1815. Fortunately, this six-storey building was bought by John Heathcoat, a lace manufacturer from Leicestershire. A gang of Luddites had attacked and wrecked his factory at Loughborough on the night of 28 June 1816 and, that summer, he transferred to Tiverton with a few salvaged frames. Loyal craftsmen made the 200-mile long journey to Devonshire on foot.

The Tiverton venture proved a great success. Heathcoat was the brilliant inventor of a new bobbin-net machine, a 'kind of mechanical pillow', which could imitate real pillow lace but made it infinitely faster. With the mill had come the invaluable leat needed to drive the great water wheel to provide power and there were all too many men and women, skilled and unskilled, eager for work. By 1822 he was employing over 1,500. Heathcoat was an enlightened employer, reducing the hours of work, paying fair wages and building, at his own expense, the first West Country factory school, opened on New Year's Day, 1843. Conscious of the continuing animosity between the established Church of England and the non-conformists, his speech stressed that it was 'to educate the children of parents of all denominations'. He had kept his distribution network in Nottingham and London, and improved transport soon added to the new prosperity.

Grandiose plans, originating in the 18th century, to build a canal from Bristol via Taunton to Topsham, to avoid the long sea journey round Land's End, were in abeyance. However, in August 1814, a less ambitious project, intended to become part of the grand scheme, was realised when the first barge carrying coal, on what was intended to be a spur line to Tiverton, arrived from Burlescombe. A useful volume of traffic was built up with barge-loads of limestone being hauled from the quarries at Canonsleigh to be burnt in the huge lime-kilns at Tiverton basin, so providing the basic fertiliser needed by the red-clay farmlands. But it was largely one-way traffic and canal tolls did not reach the projected levels. When a new railway station, Tiverton Junction (then called Tiverton Road), was built on the main Bristol-Exeter line and, in 1848, the branch line to Tiverton itself opened, freight fell away sharply – coal merchants who had been using the canal wharves transferred to goods yards down at the station. In 1863, competition proved too fierce for the owners and the canal was sold to the Bristol and Exeter Railway.

The railways continued to expand. The line from Tiverton to Dulverton, opened on 1 August 1884, meant that the way through to the northern reaches of the Exe Valley and the moor beyond was now clear. Finally, the Exe Valley Railway, south to Exeter, following the course of the Exe via Cadeleigh, Thorverton and Bramford Speke, was opened on 1 May 1885. Direct access to the county town led to a surge of business in both directions, a huge influx of farmers on market days, 'crocodiles' of school boys and girls, shoppers and visitors.

The canal, by now, was moribund. The limestone traffic continued but serious leaks made the section near Halberton unserviceable in 1921 and again in 1924. All traffic stopped. The canal had been sold on to the Great Western Railway who leased it out mainly for the culling of water-lilies for flower markets. It grew more and more neglected – though not by local fishermen who found good sport in the coarse fishing. From the G.W.R., it passed to the British Railways Board, then to the British Transport Commission. There was always a danger that it would be filled in but local protest groups secured a reprieve in 1966, and in 1971 it was made over to Devon County Council who designated it a Country Park. Today horses again plod along the towpath drawing the *Tivertonian* and the *Hyades*, traditional brightly-coloured barges, packed with visitors of all ages, through the unspoilt woods and pasturelands.

Tiverton was thriving. The census of 1831 had shown it to be the third largest town in Devon with a population nearing 10,000 – though still a long way behind Plymouth, the largest, with around 79,000 and Exeter with 32,000. At last, too, with the Reform Bill of 1832, the aspirations of Tivertonians to have a voice in the affairs of the nation were realised. Not surprisingly, John Heathcoat topped the poll in December 1832 and as one of the two first Members rode in triumphal procession through the town, attended by outriders, drums and fifes, the clubs with their banners, females in the employ of Mr. Heathcoat, four abreast, and a band. In 1835, he was joined by another popular figure, Lord Palmerston, who kept his safe seat until his death in 1865. They were from opposite ends of the social spectrum: Heathcoat, the son of a grazier, born in the village of Duffield, near Derby, was one of the new breed of self-made men, a brilliant inventor-industrialist with business acumen and enough languages to enable him to establish subsidiaries in France (St Quentin) and Sicily (Messina). Palmerston was born into the ruling class; he never earned a penny, didn't bother with foreign tongues but he, too, was committed to the new radicalism. The partnership was a great success – Palmerston, the cabinet minister and Prime Minister, working with Heathcoat, the back-bencher; Palmerston sending out gun-boats, Heathcoat dealing with constituents' problems. Tiverton took both men to their hearts; whenever 'Pam' came to Tiverton and addressed the townspeople from the windows of the *Three Tuns*, wild cheers echoed around the valley. When Heathcoat died, in 1861, the town put up the shutters and laid a carpet of black cloth the length of the road from his house at Bolham to St Peter's.

With the new-found prosperity, money was available for many projects; two 'under-privileged' districts came into their own. Over the bridge, in West Exe, the home of many of the factory workers, St Paul's, a well-proportioned mid-Victorian church with an impressive spire, was completed in 1856. This was the Church of England's answer to the threat from the Roman Catholic Chapel of St John, founded in 1837, also in West Exe and attracting local worshippers. For some years the vicar kept up an animated disputation with the priest of St John's in the local news-sheet, the *Tiverton Gazette*, first published in 1858.

A new Congregational church was built in St Peter's Street in 1832 on the site of the ramshackle Steps Meeting House which had stood there from 1687 on the site first used by the Rev. Theophilus Polwheile in 1660; John Wesley had described it as a 'dreary preaching-house'. He had first come to Tiverton to visit his brother Samuel, Headmaster of Blundell's, who died in 1739 and is buried in St George's churchyard. John made frequent visits to Tiverton, preaching at open-air meetings. On one of these visits, 29 August 1751, it was Blundell's anniversary day and Wesley was appalled by the rowdy behaviour of the visiting gentlemen and of the clergy in St Peter's. That evening, as he preached, probably in the Corn Market, a rabble of their servants 'barracked' him and he had to be hustled away. That did not deter him from returning to Tiverton, often on his way through to the mining communities of Cornwall. From the small rooms used by him in 1752, the present Methodist church which seats 700 arose in 1814. The Baptist church also was well established in Newport Street. A community, one of the five oldest in England, had been founded there around 1607 by Dutch Anabaptists. The baptismal tank was fed from the nearby town leat. A chapel on the site of the 17th-century place of worship had been completed in 1732 and this was rebuilt in 1877.

The other district to benefit was Elmore, a rough quarter on the west bank of the Lowman, with a reputation for lawlessness, drunkenness, dog-fighting, cock-fighting and badger-baiting! On 29 June 1843, the indefatigable Congregational Pastor Heudebourck, who did not hesitate to solicit funds from Palmerston himself, opened the Elmore Chapel. Carriages crowded into the street and Elmore no longer felt itself excluded from the town by its poverty and by public disapproval. The chapel is active today. Later, in 1903, Elmore Church was opened as a Mission Church of St Peter's, but it closed in 1952.

Building was also going on at St Peter's itself. There had been settlement, roof timbers had decayed, the north wall was propped up by buttresses, there were fissures in the south aisle and masonry fell from the parapets and battlements. Between 1853-6 a good part of the church was rebuilt but, in the process, many of the splendid treasures were swept away – the medieval chancel screen, the 17th-century pulpit, and the galleries which had once seated the boys of Blundell's and the Blue Coat schools. The great brass candelabrum (Queen Anne) and the sounding board of the pulpit were saved by the Rev. Rayer, Rector of Tidcombe, who took them to Holcombe Rogus; they have since been restored to St Peter's.

Education, too, was seeing great changes. In 1882, after much heart-searching, Blundell's School moved from its gracious Jacobean building beside the Lowman to a new site at Horsdon, about a mile outside town, on the road to Halberton. Here, their own school chapel was built in 1883. Here, the school could expand and thrive – boarding houses were built, there was space for playing fields and country pursuits and, at its tercentenary in 1904, it was referred to as 'the Eton of the West'.

Locally, there was still the conviction that 'forreyners' had taken over the school which Blundell had intended for the town and a famous Chancery case decided that this was, in fact, so. However, it was too late to rectify the position and Blue Coat schools had flourished since 1713 when 60 boys and, in 1714, 50 girls had been provided for in a building in St Peter's churchyard. In 1842 the schools transferred to handsome premises in Castle Street (now St Peter's Church Rooms) and, in 1909, were replaced by the Tiverton Middle Schools on the Wilderness in Barrington Street. These soon achieved a fine scholastic standing and attracted boys and girls with county scholarships from the villages and farms of the Exe Valley who would otherwise have been denied their chance of entry to the professions.

Primary education was also changing. The National schools, built in 1841 in

St Andrew's Street, were neither sectarian nor funded by charities. The arched doorways, still marked 'Boys' and 'Girls', now lead in to the Tiverton Museum which, besides a gallery housing the historic 'Tivvy Bumper' and railway memorabilia, has a forge, a lace gallery, a farmyard full of old carts and penny-farthings, and innumerable exhibitions, books, photographs and ephemera which reflect the life of Tiverton and district through the ages.

Down the street, the Gaol was built in 1846 to replace the old Bridewell; this impressive building, now two private dwellings, was given in 1977 to the Devon Historic Buildings Trust.

The face of the town itself was changing, too. On the site where the ancient chapel of St Thomas stood in 1554 and where, around 1615, the Guildhall, better known locally as the Town House, was built, the present more ornate town hall was erected in 1864. The old building had seen some of Tiverton's most dramatic events, riots included. A cellar passage led to the adjacent *Angel Inn* where, at convivial gatherings, much of the 'unofficial' business of the borough was 'arranged' in the 18th and early 19th century. The new solid Victorian edifice was much more sedate. The Council Chamber also serves as the Magistrates' Court; the ground floor, formerly the Tiverton Bank, now provides some of the offices of the Mid Devon District Council, responsible for some 61 parishes spread over approximately 353 square miles. An elegant salon, the mayoralty room is, by courtesy of the mayor, used for receptions to Tiverton's twin towns of Chinon and Hofheim. Here were welcome the Captain and men of H.M.S. *Hermes*, Tiverton's adopted Royal Navy ship (now sold). A.G.M.s of local societies and charities are also held there.

A mile outside town, another ornate building arose on a splendid hillside. John Heathcoat's grandson, John Heathcoat Amory, who inherited the business in 1861, commissioned William Burges, the architect of Cardiff Castle, to build a country house, Knightshayes Court, near Bolham. The neo-Gothic exterior is wholly Burges's but, inside, little remains of his work except some charming corbel figures of men and animals and some splendid woodwork designed by him. Said to be too dilatory, he was replaced by J. D. Crace, who completed the decoration of the interior with the then fashionable stencilled ceilings and wall surfaces. These are being restored by the National Trust to whom Knightshayes was bequeathed by Sir John Amory who died in 1972.

'Court' was also the name on the innumerable short passages in the town leading to groups of poor houses and cottages huddled together and only accessible through these alleyways which usually passed underneath existing houses. These were a relic of the days when the serge-master or woollen manufacturer needed a large open space for a process known as 'warping the chains' and the workers' dwellings were grouped round the yard. There was no sanitation and usually only one tap for each 'court'. Often they were named after the builder or owner. Tiverton was honeycombed with these mysterious archways, reinforced with dark planking. Most have disappeared – those in West Exe when the road was widened earlier this century, and others during development. Several can still be seen, now modernised.

Transport by road was vastly improved by the abolition in 1883 of toll-gate charges. Until then, there had been a turnpike on every road leading into Tiverton and no-one on horseback and no wheeled vehicle escaped a charge, except on Sundays when there was a restricted form of exemption for those going to places of worship.

Health had not been neglected. The Tiverton Infirmary and Dispensary was founded in 1852 but served out-patients only. In 1868, additional wards were opened so that inpatients could be admitted, sparing them the long journey to Exeter. There was some poverty in Tiverton but with the factory as an industrial base and the surrounding countryside to supply relatively cheap food, there was nothing like the Dickensian misery of the big cities. Victorian prosperity, however, was not to last.

Tiverton in the Twentieth Century

The First World War (1914-18) wrought a huge change. Many men of Tiverton and many boys of Blundell's school had served in the Crimean War, in colonial skirmishes, and in the Boer War, but now the whole town was engulfed in the bitter struggle. Tiverton railway station witnessed all too many departures of young men from outlying farms and villages, driven up in pony traps to catch the last train they would take out of the Valley. Their names are recorded on wayside memorials and in lonely churches; those from Tiverton itself are to be found on the screen in the chapel at St Peter's alongside those who fell in the later, 1939-45 war, and also in the Memorial Room at the Library.

Tiverton was slow to move into the Age of the Car. Here, remote from the great car factories, the bicycle at first replaced the horse, the pony trap and Shanks' pony. The town awoke to the ringing of bicycle bells as the workers converged on the factory. An enterprising local inventor, Frederick Woodgates, met a huge demand for his inner tube puncture kit, Patchquick, manufactured in Station Road from 1910 to 1950. Every school and office had its bicycle rack.

The inter-war years were difficult for Tiverton. 'Company' shops, the International, Lipton's, Home and Colonial, the New Zealand Meat Company, their counters piled high with cheap produce from the Empire, undercut the local friendly family-run shops and drove many out of business. Other tradespeople, too, were hard hit; the Domestic Bazaar Company and Woolworth's had come to town.

Farming was in the doldrums. Although the Jarrow marchers rightly received national sympathy, the plight of smallholders and farmers was largely ignored. For many there was no dole. Some ate cheap imported margarine to sell every ounce of butter they could make; their wives raised hens and ducks and lugged heavy baskets of vegetables to market to make ends meet. Those not 'on the panel' did not qualify for medical and dental treatment and went without.

All too soon, war again claimed the young men (and this time young women) and World War Two again demanded the most resolute effort of those left behind. On the farms, land girls gave invaluable help; in the factory, workers toiled heroically long hours. Heathcoat's had always been ready to diversify. The factory moved out of lace and net when these became unfashionable into silk, rayon, crêpe, nylon and elastic net and now turned back again to produce millions of yards of fine cotton net for mosquito nettings and a coarser version for camouflage nets. These required variously coloured and shaped patches to be put on by hand to perfect the disguise and part-time workers were trained by Heathcoat's to do this at home or wherever space was available.

Over 500 workers turned to producing parachutes, complete with harness, for airborne troops and to making the special containers for 'drops' of supplies and weapons over enemy territory. Parts of aero-engines and bombs were also produced, but although traitor Haw-Haw, broadcasting for Germany, sneered that all this was known to the enemy, Tiverton remained physically unscathed. Just one enemy plane dropped six 100-lb. bombs in the Belmont Road area on the night of 31 July 1940; damage was caused but there were no casualties.

Heathcoat's had always had a foundry on site and when the manufacture of cultivators became vital, as U-boats threatened the island's food supplies, the factory quickly switched to making the scuffler type of cultivator. By 1943, it was reckoned to be the biggest manufacturer of this type.

After the war, life was never to be the same again. The internal combustion engine had come into its own. Cattle transport lorries now brought animals to market; the busy farm dogs, once consigned to a special dog pound in the market, became redundant. Crocodiles of children no longer trooped up and down Barrington Hill on their way to school from the station; they came in by special bus. The number of public houses declined drastically. Once there was said to have been a different pub for every day of the month; now, one by one, they were closing, although the concession of all-day opening on Tuesdays lingered on in deference to the thirsty market traders. Tradesmen no longer lived in the spacious rooms above their shops; they moved out to new suburbs, Broomhill, Wilcombe, Cotteylands, Cowley Moor, Post Hill. The town streets were deserted at night. The brewery was taken over by Whitbread's and closed; their bottling plant moved to West Exe.

Development was visible everywhere. The East Devon Technical College arose on the Bolham Road site where previously huts had housed Italian prisoners-of-war. Tiverton Modern School nearby was expanded into a comprehensive school; the old Grammar schools were allotted to younger children. A new church, St Andrew's, was built near Blundell's to serve the nearby suburbs of Cowley Moor and Wilcombe. A new coach and car park at Phoenix Lane encroached on the town centre.

In 1974 Tiverton bitterly felt that it had lost its identity. Although retaining its mayor and town council, it became, under the reorganisation of boroughs and parishes into larger units, a part, with Bampton, Crediton and Cullompton, of the Mid Devon District Council. Wryly, a signboard at one entrance to the town proclaims 'Former Borough of Tiverton'. The town mourned the loss of its independence; local sense of history and civic pride had always been strong.

Again, in 1988, Tiverton feared for its identity. The North Devon Link Road was driven through the northern outskirts to provide access from the M5 to the north Devon coast towns of Barnstaple and Bideford. This called for a new bridge spanning the historic Exe. The Town-of-the-Two-Fords feared it would be overwhelmed – or by-passed ...

The Town of the Two Fords

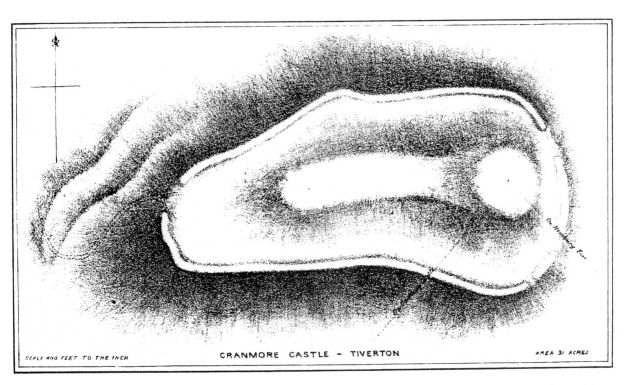

SCALE 400 FEET TO THE INCH   CRANMORE CASTLE - TIVERTON   AREA 31 ACRES

1. Cranmore Castle. Not the usual 'castle' but the west-country name for a fortified hill-camp. In a commanding position on Skrinkhills, high above the Exe and Lowman, it was once occupied by the tribe of the *Dumnonii* whose headquarters were at Exeter. It may have been part of a chain of communications with Hembury Fort and Cadbury Castle.

2. Cadbury Castle (to left, not visible) towers above St Michael's. Five miles from Tiverton, the 829 ft.-high Iron Age earthwork dominates the Exe valley. It is said to be inhabited by a dragon and is believed to hide buried treasure – 'If Cadbury Castle and Dolbery Hill down delven were; Then Denshire might plow with a golden Coulter and eare with a gilded shere'.

3. Nothing was known of Roman Tiverton until 1946 when aerial archaeology revealed a faint soilmark on the hillside at Bolham (near Knightshayes). At first it was believed to be a marching camp but excavations (1981-6) showed it to be a regular fort, dating from *c*.A.D. 50, where some 500 men of the Augusta II Legion, then occupying Exeter, would have been stationed. This model, in Tiverton museum (given 1989), shows the probable appearance of the west gate: pottery, broken roof tiles, beads, a ring and an intaglio were found.

4. St Peter's church, high above the Exe. Consecrated in 1073 by Leofric, first bishop of Exeter, it probably replaced a wooden Saxon place of worship on the same site. The tower dates from *c*.1400. The Exeleigh footbridge, a valued east-west short cut, was damaged by 1960 floods and not replaced.

5. St Peter's: the Norman doorway in the north wall. The deep zig-zag arch is made of volcanic stone which is locally called trap and probably came from Washfield or Thorverton. It was possibly the entrance for the lords of the nearby castle.

6. Tiverton Castle. Henry I, fearful of an uprising, commanded Richard de Redvers (de Riparys and de Rivers are alternative spellings), his 'faithful and beloved Councillor', to build this stronghold high above the Exe. It was impregnable – until the Civil War. When the de Redvers line died out, the castle descended to the Courtenays.

7. Tiverton Castle ruins, showing part of the curtain wall and the chapel (thought to be the building on the right, immediately above the Exe). Somewhere here, an underground tunnel gave an escape route, probably emerging in Fore Street, to ensure that horsemen and troops could be summoned to help in time of trouble.

8. Bickleigh Castle, unusually, was not sited defensively high above the Exe, but hidden in the woods on its banks, below Bickleigh Bridge. This Norman moated castle is mentioned in Domesday. A Royalist stronghold, it surrendered to Fairfax during the Civil War and its fortifications, except the gate house and south wing, were demolished.

9. Bickleigh Castle: the armoury. The suits of armour, breast-plates, cannon and cannon balls, cross-bows and pikes are all authentic and the Cromwellian suit of armour is typical of that worn by the Roundheads under Fairfax who stormed the castle. Fairfax was encamped nearby, at Cadbury Castle.

10. Bickleigh Court, c.1900: the ivy-clad ruins of a once-proud castle. In the 16th century it was reconstructed by the Carews, but by Victorian times it had degenerated into a farmhouse. In 1922 it was rescued and has been well restored.

11. Bickleigh Castle: the 12th-century thatched chapel, said to be the oldest complete building in Devon. It has a medieval stained-glass window, an Early English font, a sanctuary ring on the west door and folding Cromwellian chairs. These were stacked against the walls so that the aged and sick could take them and sit down ('the weaker to the wall'). The congregation stood for church services.

12. The Exe in spate – the great flood of 1960. This is typical of the many years when West Exe was overwhelmed by the surging waters. After the floods of 1952 (the year of the Lynmouth disaster) a flood wall was built but the water swept over and submerged the factory whose two chimneys can be seen in the background.

13. The Lowman rising. Lowman Green was Tiverton's 'Speakers' Corner'; members of the Salvation Army regularly played and spoke under the lamp-post on the right. Here, *c.*1920, the river is making its voice heard; it is lapping the bridge and soon the coal and Great Western Railway carts will have to ferry people east of the bridge and from the railway station into town.

Wool and Wealth

14. Greenway's Almshouses in Gold Street, founded in 1517 for five poor aged men. Badly damaged in the 1731 fire, the Tudor chapel survived almost unscathed. Below the carved cornice is the injunction 'Have grace, ye men, and ever pray/For the sowl of John and Jone Greenway'.

15. Brass rubbings of John and Joan Greenway in St Peter's church. As befits a wealthy merchant and member of the great guilds, John is wearing a long fur-lined gown with full sleeves. A penner and inkhorn hang from his girdle. His wife, Joan, has a high-peaked and embroidered head-dress, tight-sleeved gown and deep fur cuffs. From her rich girdle hangs a chain with a pomander and jewel.

16. The Greenway chapel, St Peter's. Completed in 1517, it was the gift of John Greenway, one of Tiverton's 'merchant princes'. The exterior carvings depict, sailing on realistic waves, the ships which made his fortune. They are armed merchantmen which carried his cloth, hides and tin, and returned with wine, dyes and miscellaneous cargoes.

Tiverton Staple Mark
Copied from the Screen in St Peters Church

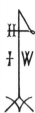

The Staple Mark of **John Waldron** *Merchant Copied from his Almshouses in Wellbrook. The Staple mark on his tomb in St Peters Church bears date 1579.*

The Staple mark of **John Greenway** *Merchant Copied from an ancient Deed bearing date the 25 September. 22nd Henry 8th — Greenways Staple is also frequently repeated in the Cornice of his Chapel both internal and external on the Capitals of some of the Pillars in St Peters Church on the Screen and on his Almshouse Chapel.*

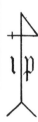

The Staple mark of **John Prowse** *Merchant Who died 3rd September 1585 Copied from his grave stone in St Peters Church.*

17. Staple marks of Tiverton merchants, 1579-1644. These identification marks had to be affixed to all merchandise carried out of the kingdom and, by law, first brought to the staple towns of which the nearest to Tiverton was Exeter. The 'logo' was based upon the Cross, said to signify that the merchant, whose initials were also incorporated, entered on his commercial dealings under the 'Banner of his Saviour'.

18. The great fire (frying pan fire) of Tiverton, 1598. The contemporary pamphlet describes how the 'chiefe Market for Cloth, that is in all the West parts of England: pleasantlye situate upon the cleere running Ryver of Exe' was reduced to ashes in a short hour, and prophetically warns London, 'the chiefe Lady-cittie of this Land', to beware of 'the like plague' (which, in the event, befell her on 2 September 1666).

The true lamentable discourse of the burning of Teuerton in Deuon=shire, the third day of April last past about the houer of one of the Clocke in the After=noone, being Market Day, 1598.

At what time there was consumed to Ashes about the Number of 400 houses, with all the Money and goods that was therein : and Fyftie persons burnt aliue through the vehemencie of the same Fyer.

AT LONDON,

Printed by THOMAS PURFOOT for THOMAS MILLINGTON, and are to be sould at his Shop in Corn Hill, under **St. Peters Church.**

19a. Waldron's Almshouses were erected for eight old men *c.*1579 in Wellbrook, West Exe. Waldron was a wool merchant who had traded extensively with Ireland and Spain. The building has many pious injunctions. Over the doorways on the ground floor are the words 'Depart thy goods whyl thou hast tyme/After thy deathe they are not thyne/God sav Queene Elizabeth'.

19b. Waldron's bell. This 450-year-old bell was bought, probably second-hand, by John Waldron on one of his business trips to the continent. It bears a small relief of the Virgin and Child and a rose on the waist. The inscription in Old Dutch reads 'In the year 1539 Aelbert Hachman cast me in Cleve. Jesus, Mary, Anne'. Cleve, the birthplace of Henry VIII's wife, Anne of Cleves, is now in West Germany, near the Dutch border. Aelbert Hachman was a famous bellfounder there and this is thought to be the only example of his work in England. Housed in the tiny 15 ft. square chapel, it has not rung out for over a century, as renovations in the 19th century left the bellcote too cramped. Thanks to the discovery of a volcanic stone quarry at Thorverton, the original purple and mauve stone of the chapel can now be matched and current restoration includes the bellcote.

20. Slee's Almshouses (right), which are still lived in, and the Great House. This was one of 44 different bequests made by wool millionaire, George Slee, who died in 1613. 'Six poore, aged Widdowes or Maidens, of the Town or Parish of Tyverton ... of the age of threescore yeres at the least' were to be the beneficiaries. He probably made the bequest in memory of his daughter, Eleanor who, at the age of 14, was a victim of the 1598 fire.

21. The Great House of St George, *c.*1613 – the home of George Slee, his business premises and traditionally the headquarters of the wool guild which met in the splendid upstairs drawing-room under a great plaster emblem of St George and the dragon. Its mullioned windows and screened passage flanked by the original studded doors are fine witnesses of a great Jacobean town house, probably replacing one on the same site destroyed by the 1598 fire.

22. Old Blundell's. This 'free grammar
school' was founded in 1604 by Peter
Blundell, a wealthy merchant, for the sons of
Tiverton but 'forreyners' could make up
numbers when necessary. 'Forreyners' soon
dominated the school and led to fights such
as that described in *Lorna Doone* between Jan
Ridd and Robin Snell.

23. Old Blundell's interior. The timbers
were said to have come from the wreckage of
the Spanish Armada, washed ashore on the
coast of Cornwall. Studies were academic,
centred on Latin, Greek and the Holy
Scriptures. The school has now been
converted into private apartments.

24. & 25.   Old Blundell's: the porter's lodge. Here lived 'Old Cop' and his kindly wife. When the Lowman flooded, 'Old Cop' erected grooved boards to make a barrier. Outside were white stones inscribed 'P B' for Peter Blundell. Blackmore relates in *Lorna Doone* that, traditionally, boys could claim a holiday when the Lowman rose over the stones.

26. Chilcott's School, St Peter's Street. The legend reads 'ROBERT COMIN ALS CHILCOT, BORNE
IN THIS TOWN, FOUNDED THIS FREE ENGLISH SCHOOLE, AND INDOWD IT WITH
MAINTENANCE FOR EVER. ANNO DNI 1611'. A nephew of Peter Blundell, he envisaged basic
education rather than classical studies. This unspoilt relic of Jacobean architecture closed as a school in
1906 and is now used for meetings of the Mid Devon District Council.

WOFVLL NEWES,

From the West-parts of England,

𝔅eing the lamentable 𝔅urning of the 𝔗owne of

TEUERTON, IN DEUONSHIRE,

Vpon the fift of August last, 1612,

*Whereunto is annexed, the former burning of the aforesaid Towne,
the third of Aprill, 1598.*

𝔏ondon:

Printed by T. S. for Thomas Pauier, 1612.

27. The second great fire, 1612 (dog-fight fire at Patey's, the dyers). The pamphlet shows the primitive fire-fighting equipment, leathern buckets and grappling irons then in use. Because of this fire, James I granted Tiverton its first royal charter on 10 August 1615, for 'the better ordering and government of the town'.

28. (*Right*) The first seal of Tiverton, granted by James I with the royal charter of 1615, depicts brilliantly the town encircled by its two rivers. Lapped by the waters of the Exe and Lowman, the houses rise steeply northwards.

29. (*Below*) Today's seal, right, is little changed from that granted with the George I replacement and renewal charter, left. Appropriately, these seals incorporate a woolsack, and the church and castle are now shown dominating the town. The Exe, left, and Lowman, right, flow under their bridges (the Exe bridge bigger) to meet south of the town.

30. (*Above left*) The mayor's pew, St Peter's. Tiverton was very proud of its status as a borough conferred by the royal charter of 1615, and embellished the pew with richly coloured figures of a lion bearing the Tudor rose and the unicorn bearing a thistle beneath the crown (a subtle compliment to James I of England, who was also James VI of Scotland).

31. (*Above right*) Cromwell Charter, 1655. This was discovered by Tiverton solicitors at Gotham House when turning out before the restoration of their Georgian building, and was then given to the museum. It attributes the terrible fires of 1598 and 1612 to the profanation of the Sabbath by local people preparing on that day for Monday's market, and so changes market day to Tuesday.

The Civil War and After

32. Tidcombe Hall (now the Marie Curie home) stands on a sacred site of great antiquity – here stood the chapel of Tidcombe Rectory for which Bishop Stafford granted a licence in 1400. John Newte, the rector, was cruelly persecuted and the rectory burnt down by the Cromwellians. After rebuilding, it was occupied for nearly 200 years by the scholarly and courageous Newte family, rectors of Tidcombe, who gave their name to the great hill leading to Cullompton.

The taking of

TIVERTON,

WITH THE

Caftle, Church, and Fort,

BY

Sir Thomas Fairfax,

ON THE

Lords-Day laft, Octob.19. 1645.

Wherein was taken

Colonel Sir *Gilbert Talbot*, the Governour.	200. Common Souldiers.
	Foure Peece of Ordnance.
Major *Sadler*, Major to Col.*Talbot*.	500.Armes, with ftore of Ammunition, Provifi-
20.Officers of note.	on, and Treafure.

ALSO

The feverall Defeats given to *Goring*, by his Excellency, and all *Gorings* Forces fled before him.

Publifhed according to Order.

LONDON,
Printed for *R. A.* *Octob.* 23. 1645.

33.   This pamphlet gives an eye witness account of the taking of Tiverton castle, church and fort by Sir Thomas Fairfax. Puritans were resolutely opposed to breaking the Sabbath, but we read that 'on this day being the Lords day Octob 19 ... all our Cannon began to play about seven a clocke in the morning, against the Castle'. It concludes 'Lieutenant-Generall Cromwell ... cometh on verie hard marches to joyne with the Generall. Gorings Horse are marched towards Plymouth'.

34a. & 34b. St Michael's, Cadbury, which lies on the south-west slope of the 829 ft. pre-Roman fortified hilltop, Cadbury Castle. Fighting was rife up and down the Exe valley, and a tombstone set in the floor commemorates George ffursdon, who was killed in action while fighting for the king at the siege of Lyme Regis, 16 March 1643.

35. *The White Horse*, Gold Street. In August
1643, a mob stoned the king's dragoons here
and an 'obstreperous Puritan miller', John
Lock, 'was taken and executed, at the sign of
the White Horse, on the north side of Gold
Street. After which the town was plundered'.
Cromwell is reputed to have stayed at the
inn later.

36. *The Lamb*, in Newport Street, opposite
St Peter's, was one of Tiverton's oldest inns.
The lamb could be a paschal lamb or signify
that the important sheep market was held
here. Like *The Palmerston* (*Three Tuns*), *The
Angel* and *The Boar's Head*, this historic inn is
now closed.

37. & 38. St Peter's church organ, 1696, built with funds raised by John Newte, rector of Tidcombe. It was the work of Christian Schmidt, nephew of Bernard Schmidt who built the organ in St Paul's Cathedral for Christopher Wren. 'It will Regulate the untunable Voices of the Multitude and ... stir up the Affections of Men, and make them fitter for Devotion.' The heads of cherubs carved on the case of the organ and the trumpeters holding up mitres on top of the organ are thought to be the work of Grinling Gibbons who worked in St Paul's Cathedral with Bernard Schmidt. Mendelssohn's wedding march was first played on this organ in March 1837 by Samuel Wreay.

39.   The great candelabrum was given to St Peter's church in 1707 by Nathaniel Thorne. It was thrown out during the Victorian restoration, 1854-6, but rescued by William Rayer, rector of Tidcombe, and taken to Holcombe Rogus. A gilded dove surmounts the branched candles. It was recently returned to the church.

40.   St Peter's before the Queen Anne candelabrum was returned. On the left, behind the light globes, is 'The Angel Delivering St Peter from Prison', given in 1784 as an altarpiece by Richard Cosway, the son of a Blundell's master. Richard was the acclaimed miniaturist of the day and he and his talented wife, Maria, were lionised by London society.

41. Tiverton market cross in Fore Street, *c*.1783. The previous cross, erected in 1649 and destroyed by the 1731 fire, was replaced by a generous merchant, Mr. Upcott. In 1685 the head of a dissenting minister, executed on the orders of the ruthless Judge Jeffreys after the Monmouth Rebellion, was affixed to it. One of the arches is now part of Heal's, the hardware shop in Bampton Street.

42. *The Palmerston Hotel*, originally *The Three Tuns*, has played an important part in the town's social and political history. In the 18th century, the mayor and corporation repaired there on the slightest pretext. In the 19th century it was renamed *The Lord Palmerston* after Tiverton's famous M.P. and Prime Minister, who at election times addressed the townspeople from the hotel windows.

43. Hogarth ticket for Blundell's anniversary,
1740. The founding of the school was marked for
many years by the boys walking to St Peter's for a
sermon. The Old Boys would dine at *The Three Tuns*
and hold a ball at *The Angel* or the Town House.
This is one of Hogarth's smaller productions, and
the ticket shows Minerva pointing to the school.

44. Bampfylde Moore Carew (1690-1758) was the
son of a rector of Bickleigh and a notorious Old Boy
of Blundell's who, following an unhappy incident
with his hounds at harvest time, ran away from
school and joined the gypsies. So charismatic was
his personality that they elected him their king. His
exploits as a trickster led to his being transported to
Maryland but he escaped back to England and, in
1745, followed Bonnie Prince Charlie to Derby.
Eventually he returned to Bickleigh – he is buried
in the churchyard there.

Political Awakening

ST GEORGE'S TIVERTON

45. St George's. It was feared that a new Act of Uniformity would lead to overcrowding at St Peter's, so the foundation stone for this new church was laid in 1714. George I's accession removed this threat and the building became a wool warehouse for Oliver Peard until it was finally consecrated in 1733.

46. St George's interior, showing the stained glass window with the cross of St Andrew, the design for which was taken from a window in Wells Cathedral.

47.　The Corn Market. This handsome seven-pillared building was constructed in 1699. At that time the bell tower had a wooden spire, burnt down in the third disastrous fire of 1731, the great bakehouse fire. The *London Daily Post* reported 'the Town is entirely ruined and the poor inhabitants misery is not to be expressed'. This important corn exchange helped restore the town's fortunes.

48.　Rev. John Russell (1795-1883), an Old Boy of Blundell's and vicar of Swimbridge. He was carpeted by his bishop, but was immensely popular with the hunting fraternity. He bred the original 14-inch-at-shoulder 'Parson Jack Russell' dog from Trump, a bitch he bought from a milkman at Oxford. The full-size dog, not the short-legged, vigorous little dog popularly known as the Jack Russell, is shortly to be recognised by the Kennel Club.

49. Tiverton's first purpose-built mill. The wool trade was in a deep depression at the end of the 18th century and this was to have been a cotton mill but, under-used, it was bought by John Heathcoat. It was the tallest building in Tiverton and dominated West Exe.

50. John Heathcoat's mill, 1825. Here he installed his newly-invented bobbin-net machine, and hundreds of people in the town and surrounding villages found employment in the factory or in supplying it. Life in Tiverton was transformed.

51. The Pannier Market opened in 1830 on the site of the old bowling green; until then markets had been held in the streets. In 1831, pens for cattle, sheep and pigs were provided at the Newport Street end. After the war, these went to Tiverton Junction (now superseded by Tiverton Parkway). In the background of this picture can be seen the old fortified hill-top, Cranmore Castle.

52. John Heathcoat (1783-1861). Driven from his factory at Loughborough, Leicestershire, when the Luddites broke up his machines, he set up again at Tiverton where his brilliant invention, the new bobbin-net machine, together with a willing workforce, quickly brought success.

53. The great water wheel. It took 60 horses to draw this 80-ton water wheel the 200 miles from Manchester to Tiverton in 1824. It had 40 wooden blades, and was 25 ft. in diameter and 50 ft. wide. It produced the equivalent of 100 horse-power at a speed of 3½ revolutions a minute and was said to coin a sovereign with every turn.

54. Heathcoat's steam plough. Heathcoat established an iron foundry and invented a steam-operated plough. It weighed 30 tons and had caterpillar tracks, an innovation some 80 years before the invention of the tank. Patented in 1832, the prototype passed early tests and demonstrations but, in 1837, sank without trace overnight in the peaty bog of Lochar Moss, near Dumfries.

55. Heathcoat's registered trade mark. Heathcoat's ingenious device for making lace on machines was patented in 1808 and won praise from contemporary engineers such as Brunel. Unscrupulous competitors infringed his patents and an expensive and widely publicised law suit won him substantial damages.

56. Model lace machine – an exact replica of the machine which enraged the Luddites who were so afraid of losing their jobs that they broke up 56 machines at Loughborough. Heathcoat was offered £10,000 compensation provided he set up again in Leicestershire, but he refused the condition and loyal workers, with a few salvaged machines, trekked to Tiverton.

57. The factory school founded by Heathcoat in 1843, nearly 30 years before the first compulsory Education Act. Children were not employed in the factory until they were 10 years old and could read and write. Conscious of the animosity between the Established Church and nonconformists, Heathcoat ruled that his school was to educate the children of parents of all denominations.

The Victorian Age

Rev. W. H. Heudebourck.

58. The Rev. William Heudebourck, 1830. An outstanding pastor of the Congregational chapel, he won respect from all classes. When the High Church refused membership of their provident society to the poor (it added a shilling a year to savings) unless they attended church, he started a rival clothing society 'for assisting the Poor without distinction of Sect or Party'.

59. Elmore Congregational church. Elmore was a very rough and neglected area, but Heudebourck first involved a 'Friday Night Company' of young people in raising money for building the chapel and then went himself to London seeking funds. He declared 'Elmore has been written on my Heart', and the triumphant opening took place on 29 June 1843.

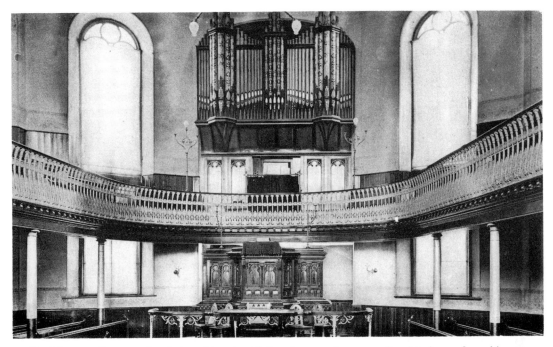

60. Tiverton Congregational chapel interior. Before the war, the nonconformist places of worship were designated 'chapel' and not dignified with the word 'church'. The chapel here is pleasing and colourful and the balcony provided added space. Today, this is the United Reformed church.

61. St Andrew Street National School, 1859. This replaced the original 1818 'Green' school, named from the green gowns supplied to the girls for whose education it was intended, which was situated on the opposite side of St Andrew Street. It is now the museum and the original 'Green' school became the Bible Christian church, now the Bethel chapel.

62. The 'neo-Venetian' Victorian town hall, erected in 1864 on the site of the ancient Guildhall or Town House where stormy sessions of the corporation were held in the 18th century. Although now one of the four towns of the Mid Devon District Council, Tiverton retains its mayor and council. They sit here in the council chamber, which also serves as the magistrates' court.

63. The drinking fountain in People's Park, given in 1888 by the Rev. George Hadow, rector of Tidcombe. The storks (some say pelicans) have lost their heads, but generations of thirsty Tiverton children were grateful for its cold water.

64. Heathcoat's outing to Teignmouth, 1854 – a painting 'presented to John Heathcoat Amory Esq by the Mechanics, operatives and others in the employ of Messrs J Heathcoat & Co to mark their high esteem of him for his conduct on all occasions as a Master but particularly on 10 August 1854 for identifying himself in assisting to carry out the regulations for the excursion to Teignmouth, the expense of which The Firm so handsomely defrayed'. The presentation was made on 12 September 1854.

65. Starkey, Knight & Ford's brewery was a major employer in the late 19th and early 20th centuries. The company was an amalgamation of Starkey (North Petherton, 1797), Knight (Bridgwater, 1840), and Thomas Ford of Tiverton, who brought 40 public houses to the new group in 1895. Taken over by Whitbread's in 1962, the company later moved to West Exe.

66.   The People's Park, opened in 1888 by the benefactor John Coles. St Peter's can be seen in the distance. The park was the scene of festivals, sports, fairs and band concerts. The elegant bandstand, with wrought-iron balustrade and tesselated floor, has been pulled down.

67.   The historic *Angel Hotel*, *c.*1900, where the Georgian corporation foregathered to 'fix' much of the town's business. Here Mayor Webber was attacked and forced to sign a paper under duress in 1765. He reneged and serious riots followed. The *Angel*'s cab seen in the courtyard was blue and black to distinguish it from the rival *Palmerston*'s yellow and black vehicle.

68. After much debate, Blundell's moved in 1882 to Horsdon on the road to Halberton. Here, there was room for expansion and boarding houses were built. Tiverton regarded the move as a betrayal of Blundell's will. The steeple on the chapel was later replaced by a tower.

69. Blundell's school chapel interior.

70. Knightshayes' gardens, laid out by eminent Victorian landscape gardener Edward Kemp (1817-91), were little changed until the 1950s. The exception was the fox and hounds topiary atop the east side yew hedges, cut in the 1920s. Hounds chase the fox all round the hedgetops and are a reminder of the family's love of hunting. The fox (right) is, literally, up against it.

71. Tally-ho! – the topiary hound nearest to the fox. His bushy tail makes him look more like the fox!

72. A Devonshire hunting family: hunting was part and parcel of country life in the 19th and early 20th centuries. Left to right: Ian H. Amory, Master of Foxhounds; C.R.S. Carew, Master of Harriers; Sir John Amory, Bart.; Ludovic H. Amory; Capt. H.H. Amory, Master of Staghounds. Hunting was available every weekday, except Tuesday (market day), and the thrills of the chase were reported in the *Tiverton Gazette*.

73. Knightshayes Court: an early aerial photograph showing the neo-Gothic house, before the conservatory was added on the left, surrounded by dark and menacing woods. *The Hound of the Baskervilles* was filmed here, mainly because one of the heraldic emblems chosen for the Amory coat of arms is a talbot, the now extinct great white hunting hound which is prominently featured in the house.

74. Knightshayes Court *c.*1890. The original façade was by William Burges, who was replaced in 1875 by John Crace, commissioned to tone down plans by the irrepressible Burges for an exuberant interior featuring stained glass, painted furniture, mosaics and sculptures.

75. Seventeenth-century boot or slipper bath from Bridwell, Uffculme, home of the Clarke family from 1610 onwards. A pipe leads down from funnel to toe to avoid the occupant being scalded by added water. Marat is said to have been murdered by Charlotte Corday in a similar bath in 1793. Soon the hip or bungalow bath took over. All were filled and emptied by hand.

76. St Catherine's, Withleigh, built 1844-47 by the Carpenter family who farmed the Withleigh (Bradley) lands for some centuries. One of the Exe valley group of churches, it serves a farming community – Withleigh Young Farmers' Club was among the first in the country. It stands on the site of a former chapel dedicated in July 1400 by Bishop Stafford which, typically, did not survive the troubled times of the Reformation.

77. Lord Palmerston, 'Pam', one of Tiverton's Liberal M.P.s, 1835-65. He was twice prime minister (1855-58 and from 1859 until his death in 1865) and was immensely popular, not least because his horses ran in the 'Tiverton Races' and he made no distinction of class or religion. The name of *The Three Tuns* was changed to *The Lord Palmerston* in his honour.

78. Frederick Temple (1821-1902), a day boy at Blundell's. Academically brilliant and universally loved and respected, he was successively Bishop of Exeter, 1869, and of London, 1885, and finally Archbishop of Canterbury in 1897. In 1901 he placed the crown on the head of Edward VII who helped the 80-year-old man, wearing heavy robes, to rise.

79. Bampton Street, *c.*1910, the main road out of Tiverton heading north to Bampton, Dulverton and the North Devon coast ports. Traffic is brisk and the road will soon have the dust laid by the municipal water-cart.

80. Unveiling the statue of King Edward VII on Lowman Green, 1912. Donated by Thomas Ford, founder of Starkey, Knight and Ford, Tiverton's brewery, it is dedicated to 'Edward the Peacemaker'.

81. Maypole dancing to celebrate Queen Victoria's Diamond Jubilee, 1897. May Day, 29 May, was declared a 'holy day' after the Restoration. It was honoured in Tiverton by a curious custom. A hideous blackened figure, 'Joe Rouser' ('Old Oliver' – Cromwell) was led about on a long rope by 'Tatey Digger'. He continually attacked the great litter of oak boughs carrying 'Charles', a little three-year-old boy, only to be driven off by his guards, dressed in white and bedecked with coloured ribbons. The crowd would pelt Joe Rouser with mud and turf and he would retaliate with the contents of a bag of soot and dirt tied around his neck. The fun was fast and furious and only a 'fine' spared Joe's victims.

Blundell boys, too, kept the feast day, 'sporting the oak' and sallying out at dawn to hack down great branches of oak and may blossom in which they buried their Upper School. A canopy of oak was suspended over a beam and from under this each boy had to 'spout', that is, recite, a piece of poetry of not less than 20 lines. Afternoon sports followed.

82. May queens were chosen, not just for the town, but also for the Girls' School, where they were the equivalent of head girls. Young Bernard Knight will be the train-bearer and his sister, Mary, will hold the cushion on which rests a beautiful crown of apple blossom.

83. Otter hunting. However barbaric it may seem today, after the saga of *Tarka the Otter*, otter hunting was a ritual part of life in the Exe valley. Here, a trophy is held aloft as the hounds hurry to the scene.

84. Otter hounds near Tiverton. Among the most famous was the Culmstock pack, founded early in the century by Mr. Jewell Collier, lord of the manor of Culmstock. The Exe valley was an ideal hunting ground as otters abounded in the tributaries. This view is of the Lowman at Gornhay. The hunt was primarily for sport but, of course, otters did denude the waters of fish.

85. Hounds at Stoodleigh Court. Typical of the spacious country houses built in Victoria's reign, this is now home to a school, Ravenswood. Unmounted devotees would follow the hunt in elegant traps.

86.   Bradfield Hall – another large country mansion, now a Devon County Council residential boys' school. The home of a distinguished family, the Walronds, it was resurrected from a near ruin in the middle of this century to become a splendid house in beautiful grounds and was the scene of numerous fêtes and garden parties, often Primrose League gatherings.

87. Goodland's coal merchants, who are still in business. The Goodland yards backed on to the railway station. Their wagons and those of adjacent coal merchants, Carpenter & Son, were a familiar sight on G.W.R. goods trains. The horse on the left has stopped at one of Tiverton's many horse troughs. Barrington and Angel hills were very steep for horses and often the iron drag had to be clamped on and additional horses sent for.

88. Thorne's the ironmongers, c.1900. This old-established business advertised its wares visually, in the old way, with a giant golden knife and fork, seen over the main doorway. Their rivals, Webber and Saunders, also now closed, surmounted their nearby entrance in Fore Street with a great plough. Most corner shops are rounded, as here, sometimes known as 'Boyce's corners' after the Victorian architect.

Telephone No. 14.

William Thorne,

Limited,

Wholesale & Retail General Furnishing and Household

✠✠✠✠✠✠✠✠✠✠✠✠✠✠✠✠✠✠
Ironmongers.

The **SHOW ROOMS,** ⌀⌀⌀
Thirty in number, are full of
Every Variety of Goods con-
nected with the Trade. ⌀⌀⌀

ALL GOODS SOLD FOR CASH
AT STORE PRICES.

AN INSPECTION IS RESPECTFULLY SOLICITED.

◉✦◉

The Central Stores, Tiverton.

THOS. KIRK (Successor to MEAD & Co.),

Printer, Stationer, AND Fancy Dealer.

KIRK

SHOW ROOM SHOW ROOM

10. PRINTER and BOOKSELLER. 10.

ART NEEDLEWORK.
STERLING SILVER ARTICLES.
BEST LEATHER GOODS.

LOCAL VIEWS.
DEVONSHIRE POTTERY
PICTURE FRAMING.

BOOKBINDING.

FORE STREET (Nearly opposite Market Entrance), TIVERTON.

89. Thomas Kirk, *c.*1900. An up-market bookshop and printer of the invaluable pocket-sized Tiverton railway timetables. The lower left-hand poster advertises tickets for a Cinderella dance at Mr. Williams' Room in St Peter Street, 9 p.m. to midnight. These were all the rage among the young set, excluded from the 'upper-crust' dances and balls, from 10 p.m. to 3 a.m. with champagne supper.

90. Locomotive No. 58, around the 1840s. One of the Bristol and Exeter Railway Company's engines which started to run to Tiverton from Tiverton Road (Tiverton Junction) in 1848 on Brunel's broad gauge lines. They were converted to standard gauge for the opening of the Exe Valley line in 1884. Beeching's axe closed the Junction line to passengers in 1964 and the Exe Valley line in 1963.

91. Locomotive No. 3794 taking on water at Tiverton station. The purchase of the canal had given the railway a useful source of water which supplied the station's water tower. This 'pannier' type engine was known locally as a 'matchbox'.

92. The 'Tivvy Bumper' No. 1442 in its last shed, the railway gallery at Tiverton museum. Lord Amory bought the engine and presented it to the town. Before its removal, it stood in the old timber yard on Blundell's Road.

93. Drinking fountain dated 1890 from Tiverton station, now in the museum together with other railway memorabilia.

94. Skating on the river Exe, 1895. The canal was more frequently frozen over and could be skated for its full length if care was taken under bridges. In 1683 the Exe was frozen over for 10 weeks, 'enabling men, women and children to pass from Westexe to the town' (Harding, Tiverton's historian).

95. Merry-go-round at a Bradfield fête, with ladies riding side-saddle. Most years a travelling fair would come to Tiverton – a steam engine also provided the power for the organ.

96.   Locomotive No. 1451, sister to the Tivvy Bumper, seen here steaming into West Exe Halt, often ran on the legendary Hemyock branch line from Tiverton Junction. Because of the tight curves as the line ran alongside the river Culm, and because train crews had to get down to open and close level crossing gates, mixed trains could take an hour for the seven-mile journey through Coldharbour Halt (woollen mill), Uffculme, Culmstock and Whitehall Halt to Hemyock (giant creamery). Opened in May 1876, the line closed for passengers in September 1963 and for freight in October 1975.

97. The Tiverton Turnpike Trust exacted tolls to be used for the upkeep of the roads it controlled, 1759-1883. This photograph shows 'Gypsy Hill' or 'Bonny's Pitt Gate' tollhouse near the north entrance to the park. It 'caught' traffic from Chettiscombe and from Bampton via the old hill road (Landrake).

98. Halberton turnpike, looking towards Tiverton. Traffic from Halberton, Uplowman and Sampford Peverell would enter the town through this turnpike. It stood opposite Cowley Lodge, near the new church of St Andrew.

99. Hunt's House turnpike, at the foot of Canal Hill, with the traditional crochet-edge eaves. An important collection point for traffic coming into Tiverton from Exeter Hill and Newte's Hill, it was demolished in 1977.

100. North Devon Cottage, still standing, controlled the roads to Rackenford (on the right) and South Molton (on the left).

101. Cottey Gate tollhouse at Patches, West Exe (named after the Patch family who occupied New Place nearby). This controlled the Seven Crosses road to Bickleigh and also the old road which, before Long Drag was built in 1843, led to Rackenford, and which also branched via Baker's Hill to Cruwys Morchard and South Molton.

102. 'Jam-pot Cottage' or 'The Castle' tollgate on the Bolham Road. One of the later tollhouses, it controlled traffic using the 'new' Exe valley road from Bampton. Still occupied today, its pink-washed walls stand out by the East Devon College near the North Devon link road roundabout.

103. St John's Roman Catholic church, West Exe, founded in 1837 under the guidance of Father Moutier, priest to the Chichester family of Calverleigh. This photograph, taken earlier this century, shows the church clearly; it is now blocked in by houses.

104. St Paul's church, West Exe, completed in 1856 as an alternative to the Catholic church. Unusually for the district, it has a steeple, and the rounded doorways and dormer windows of its square and the street present a most attractive grouping of buildings.

Twentieth-century Tiverton

105. Fore Street, *c*.1900, looking east with one's back to the town hall. This, with its continuation, Gold Street, is the main street through the town, but in summer the dust had to be laid by water-carts. After heavy rain, ladies had to secure their long skirts with a special clip to keep them clear of the mud.

106. Fore Street in 1906, looking farther east to its junction with Bampton Street and its continuation, Gold Street, towards the Lowman. On the left can be seen the balcony of the Athenaeum, a gentlemen's club, later the art school. High on the roof, in front of the flagpole, can be glimpsed the splendid royal coat of arms (now in the museum).

107. Fore Street, *c.*1932, looking west towards the town hall. Company multiples were taking over from the family-run shops by this time. International Stores, the name in huge gold letters, is on the left; on the right is Lipton Ltd. Above Lipton's is a handsome building which was once the Athenaeum, a gentlemen's club where debates and dances took place. It later became the Technical, Science and Art School.

TIVERTON  DEVON

Population 9610.

Situate in the centre of the far famed

EXE VALLEY

Staghounds and Foxhounds meet regularly near the Town.

First-class 18 hole Golf Course.

Public Hard Tennis Courts.

Full Size Sea-washed Turf Bowling Green.

BLUNDELL'S SCHOOL

One Mile from the Town.

Good Railway and Bus facilities.

Within easy reach (by car) of the

DOONE VALLEY

For further particulars apply to
The Chairman of the Mercantile Association,
8, Gold Street, Tiverton;
or to the Town Clerk.

---

108. The reverse of the Fore Street town hall photograph (plate 107) bore this advertisement – a first attempt at publicity. The town's attractions then were roughly the same as today.

109. A barrel organ, now in Tiverton museum. Members of the Salvation Army are collecting outside the *Wheatsheaf Inn*, West Exe, near the factory, *c.*1905. The appeal reads 'Self-Denial Week. Kindly Assist Missionary Work'. The organ is Italian by Rossi and Spinelli and the figure on top replaces the traditional organ-grinder's monkey.

110. The Tiverton Middle Schools, founded 1909. They inherited nothing from Peter Blundell's will though he had sought to provide education for the sons of the town. The boys' part (far side) was known as Tiverton Boys' Middle School, but the girls dropped the term 'middle', though this was carved on the building, and were known by the more genteel title, The Tiverton Girls' School.

111. Water-bailing at Chettiscombe, 1905. Boys with withy wands to beat the bounds, and pioneers with axes to clear obstructions, are on their way to Norwood Common, some 7½ miles from Tiverton. Here rises the leat, or town lake, given to the town c.1250 by Isabella, Countess of Devon, to provide a stream of pure water in perpetuity for the people of Tiverton.

112.   Perambulation of the Leat (water-bailing), 1905. Setting out from the town hall to make the official declaration at nearby Coggan's Well are Mayor H. Mudford, the aldermen and councillors. Waiting in St Andrew Street are a cart-load of flour sacks from Hobby Horse Mill and, outside the Tiverton dye works, a milk cart with the ubiquitous churn.

113. Tiverton clock tower, presented by Thomas Ford in 1907. It stands on Lowman Green, an historic point of entry down the hills from Cullompton. John Penruddock and his gallant Royalist followers from Wiltshire entered this way on 12 March 1655. Their uprising was unsuccessful – Captain Croke and his Commonwealth troopers overwhelmed them at South Molton that night.

114. Staff of the Tiverton Workhouse, c.1890. Built in 1699, it was originally known as the Hospital, then the Union, later the Workhouse and, today, Belmont Hospital for the elderly. It has never had a Dickensian reputation. Standing (left to right) are the Porter, the Assistant Matron, Nurse Cashin, the Master's Clerk, and (in knee breeches) the Master, Mr W.J. Penney. Seated (left to right) are the Industrial Officer (today called the occupational therapist), Nurse Leaworthy, the Medical Officer and the Matron, Mrs. Penney. This 'Workhouse' site will probably be used for the planned major new hospital for Tiverton as the present general hospital is inadequate.

115. No hip flask, just a firkin of cider, possibly scrumpy. The horses are on a plateau, above a steep coombe at Borough Corner, at a meet of Sir John Amory's Harriers, 2 October 1907. Hares were more common then than now.

116.   Doctors enjoyed great prestige in the early part of the century. Their coachmen wore top hats, usually with a cockade, and were smartly turned out in dark uniforms with brass buttons. Here, Dr. Slack of Uffculme, more informally dressed, is on his rounds in 1900.

117.   Woodgates Bros. Frederick Woodgates had established a sizeable factory in Blundell's Road to make 'Patchquicks', the inner tube repair kit which he had invented. Later he added the sale of motor cars and accessories to his business.

118.   Little Silver, at the bottom of St Andrew's Street. Lying at the foot of Cranmore Castle and near the banks of the Lowman just before it joins the Exe, this is one of the oldest parts of the town. The cob-and-thatch cottages, typical of those that burnt like tinder in 1598, 1612 and 1731, have now given way to council houses.

119.   View from Bickleigh Bridge, looking up-river towards Tiverton. The thatched cottage on the right is still intact. It was often marooned by floods, as was the venerable *New Inn* opposite. This was the haunt of shepherds (and their dogs) in the 1900s, but is now a roadhouse, *The Trout*. The signal on the right, at danger, guards the approach to the railway bridge spanning the Exe, just before Cadeleigh station.

120. Bickleigh Bridge, the pack-horse bridge built by Hiram Arthur in the 17th century and scheduled as an ancient monument. It stands on the site of an earlier wooden bridge where, in the 14th century, Sir Alexander Cruwys of Cruwys Morchard is said to have fought and won a duel with a Carew of Bickleigh whose ghost haunts the place. Just beyond the bridge, the river tumbles down a wide weir and the splendid views of the Devonshire hills have made this a celebrated beauty spot.

Bickleigh Ford.

121. The ford at Bickleigh. Here foot passengers could cross to avoid the dangers of the narrow bridge. Although V-recesses had once been made for pedestrians to avoid the traffic, these were removed when the bridge was widened in 1772. The ford no longer exists; the far side has become part of the garden of Bickleigh Cottage.

122. Collipriest House, below the confluence of the Exe and Lowman, another beauty spot with river and woodland walks.

123. Castle Street, formerly Frog Street, Tiverton. The Leat, given *c*.1250 by Isabella, Countess of Devon, bisects the street. The tall buildings on the right are the former Blue Coat School. Founded in 1712, the school moved to these premises in 1842. After 1909, when the boys and girls moved to the new Middle Schools at the Wilderness in Barrington Street, school dinners were provided here for the train boys and girls. The buildings are now used as St Peter's church rooms.

124. Lowman Green with the clock tower and Edward the Peacemaker. The white horse is going through the archway to the stables and backyard of the *Prince Regent Inn*.

125.   Victory pageant, 1919. The history of Tiverton was celebrated in a grand pageant held in the grounds of Collipriest. Here, Henry Codrington Butler impersonates Captain Tally of the 'Tiverton Fencibles', a local corps of infantry volunteers raised at the time of the Napoleonic invasion scare. Robed civic and church dignitaries and armed horsemen featured in the story.

126.   Tiverton's very own police force of eleven regulars and two 'specials' (wearing caps). Founded *c.*1849, it was the smallest and one of the oldest borough forces in the country. In 1943 it became part of the Devon Constabulary. This photograph was taken in 1938. Back row (left to right): Special Constable Bennett, Police Constables F. Harding, S. Edwards, W. Stuckey, S. Badcock, A. Chidgey, J. Squires, and Special Constable Morrell. Front row (left to right): Acting Police Sergeant W. Land, Police Sergeant F. Galpin, Chief Constable M. Beynon, Police Sergeant F. Williams, and Police Constable C. Richards.

127. Children's carnival at Tiverton Park in 1933. Years before John Alderson, head of Devon and Cornwall Constabulary, advocated 'community policing' it was practised by Tiverton's friendly and respected 'coppers', including the 'Chief'. Mr. Viney (background left, wearing keeper's hat) lived in the keeper's house, presided over the opening and shutting of the ornate gates, and kept everything and everyone in strict but splendid order. The policemen are, from left to right, Police Constable Chidgey, Sergeant Williams and Chief Constable Beynon.

128. & 129. Agricultural shows (at the show field, now Amory Park) were red letter days for the whole valley. Judging ended with coloured rosettes and important coloured cards in every category, from cattle and poultry to butter-making, Devonshire cream (in huge mixing bowls) and flower arranging in the great marquee. Show jumping and a parade of hounds closed the day. The photograph above shows Mayor H. Mudford opening the 1907 show on Thursday 25 July. Right, Police Sergeant Williams, on a horse loaned from Knightshayes, keeps an eye on things. In those days (c.1930), police sergeants wore stripes on one arm only.

130. Lace factory, 1900. Trade was flourishing as lace and net veiling was in great demand in the Empire, especially India, and America. The factory school (right) had to be expanded to accommodate more and more girls and boys. The workforce is leaving by the wide road across the mill leat, with its classic ironwork railings (sent for scrap in World War Two).

131. Tiverton factory fire, 1936. Fire almost totally destroyed the Heathcoat factory. Times had changed. Fire engines from all the neighbouring towns raced to help, and when a much-respected Baptist minister deplored the possible effect on a town so dependent on one major industry, he was told that the town did not stand in need of charity – a far cry from the briefs of Elizabeth and James appealing for donations after the huge devastations of 1598 and 1612, and from the subscriptions raised in 1731.

132.   Aftermath of the factory fire, Sunday 6 December 1936. The ferocity of the fire caused whole floors, many carrying heavy machinery, to collapse into heaps of mangled iron.

133.   Proclamation of the Armistice, 1918. Before the age of radio and television, news of great national events was announced, with due ceremony, from the steps of the town hall. Crowds assembled – men in strawyards, trilbies, cloth caps, bowlers, even a black topper; boys in caps, one cub on the right; girls in school straws and women in brimmed hats.

134. Starkey's outing at Weymouth, 1921. Whether for factory, choir, bell-ringers, bible class, Sunday school or shops, outings were a feature of social life between the wars. Here, brewery workers are enjoying a trip to the coast. In the back of the small car and nearest the camera is Corporal Thomas Henry Sage, who was awarded the V.C. in 1917 for throwing himself on a bomb, so saving the lives of his comrades. He worked at the brewery after the war.

135. Tiverton's carnival annually raised money for the hospital. A long torchlight procession wended its way through the town, and collecting boxes on the end of long poles reached the crowded windows over the shops. Here, in 1936, the factory reeling department is having a joke at the expense of Belisha beacons.

136.   Net folding department, c.1920. Many operations were best done by the deft hands of women. At incredible speed, they would throw the net (usually silk) from side to side of the table, using the 3 ft. 'rulers' seen in the middle of the table (right) to form the fold. The light, airy 'workshop' was a friendly place.

137. Blundell's tercentenary, 1904. The procession is returning from St Peter's and crossing Lowman Bridge. It will very soon reach Old Blundell's from which the school moved to Horsdon, about a mile away, in 1882.

138. Triumphal arch erected across Gold Street in honour of Blundell's tercentenary. It bore the school motto *Pro Patria Populoque* and stretched across Gold Street from Thorne's the grocers to the steps (near left) leading down to the Pound. Near here, stray cattle, sheep and horses were impounded until claimed.

139. Tiverton railway station decorated for the tercentenary. The stationmaster (right) was then an important and dignified figure. The school brought good business to the railway, boys travelling twice termly with their trunks and other luggage.

140. Sir John Heathcoat-Amory, 1st Baronet, was given the Freedom of the Borough in 1907. He is seated left of the mayor with Lady Amory to the right. At the same ceremony, his portrait (with head!) was presented to the town. The splendid silver gilt maces, made in the city of London in 1727, are among the treasures of the 'borough'.

141. Proclamation of King Edward VIII's accession, 1936. The special platform has been erected outside the town hall and Tiverton puts on a brave show with band, military presence, and many bared heads, despite the sleet and snow.

142. Cullompton fair, just before World War One. The wide main street, the Bull Ring, provides a perfect market place. Only the sheep are penned, the red Devon cattle being roughly barricaded with a cart or two. These were real horned cows and bullocks which could (and did) toss when in the mood. After World War Two they gave way to the ubiquitous 'polled' Friesian.

143. Red cows with horns – the sort of red Devons which added their distinctive colouring to the green fields before World War Two. Aggressive when being driven through unfamiliar streets to the cattle yards at Tiverton market, they could be dangerous. Fanny Best, nursemaid, was awarded a bravery certificate for saving her charges from an attack.

144. Barrington Street, c.1925. The wide archway, surmounted by a lion's head, led to gardens and orchards stretching right through to Elmore. The big house had vast cellars, and a colporteur who distributed bibles and tracts for the Bible Society lived in the small house below. All is now demolished as far as the street-lamp but the new development, Maple Grove, still bears the lion's head.

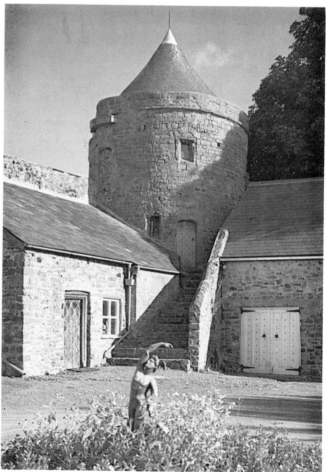

145. The castle: the restored south-east round tower. On Sunday morning, 19 October 1645, when Fairfax launched the attack at 7 a.m., the nurse to Sir Gilbert Talbot, the castle governor, was reputedly holding the baby while watching from a window here. A shot killed her, but the baby was unharmed.

GREENWAY HOUSE,

TERMS MODERATE.

DAY AND BOARDING SCHOOL,

TIVERTON.

Home for
Anglo-Indian
and
Colonial
Children.

GIRLS' DEPARTMENT :
University Examinations.

BOYS (Sons of Gentlemen)
prepared for Blundell's
and other Public Schools.

KINDERGARTEN.

Principals :

Miss MALLETT and
Miss ENGLAND,

Assisted by
a thoroughly qualified Staff.

HEALTHY SITUATION.

LARGE HOUSE.

GOOD PLAYGROUNDS AND
GARDEN.

146a. & 146b.   Greenway House, *c.*1900. The school in St Peter Street (later the *Lorna Doone Hotel*, now flats) provided for the children of those serving abroad in the far-flung British Empire. Tiverton had several such schools for 'Anglo-Indian and Colonial Children' and the sons and daughters of gentlemen. In a class-conscious society, local children were admitted rarely, and never if the family was in trade and lived over the shop.

147. Tidcombe canal bridge, *c*.1900. The first stone bridge after the canal leaves the basin, it carries the narrow Tidcombe Lane. Rushes and water lilies have taken over. The wider area on the right was dignified by the name of 'Marina' and the nearby road named Marina Way. Bungalows, with gardens running to the water's edge and the towpath, now line both banks for the first one-mile stretch.

148. Grand Western Canal at Rock Bridge where the canal passes beneath the Halberton-Sampford Peverell road. The landing stage was a wharf where stone was piled for the barges or 'tubs' to take on to Tiverton.

149. Canal near Tiverton. A lease to pick the water lilies was held by a Sampford Peverell family. The flowers went by rail to London, the Midlands and the North and were used in table decorations and wreaths. St Aubyn's Villas in the background was once the home of Tiverton's preparatory school.

150. Sampford Peverell Bridge which passes over the canal and towpath. This postcard was sent in 1910. In April 1811, 300 navvies working on the canal, many drunk, rioted. They stormed into Tiverton and, at Sampford, attacked the house of a Mr. Chave, concerned the previous year in the apparitions of the famous Sampford ghost which had plagued a village house for three years, despite all investigations and an offered reward of £250. It had attracted nationwide interest.

151.   Tiverton's first aeroplane, June 1912. This photograph shows Monsieur Calmet, the pilot, being welcomed at Knightshayes by Sir Ian Amory (left), the mayor, Mr. Alfred Gregory, the borough surveyor (holding his hand) and Chief Constable Thomas Mercer (right).   A previous French aerial descent had been made in 1786 when M. Lecroix came down in a balloon at Cadbury Castle.

152.   The Tiverton town band with bandmaster W. Loosemoore. There has always been a strong musical tradition in Tiverton, with amateur theatrical and operatic productions at the Electric Theatre, the New Hall and the schools. The prize-winning town band played at most important municipal functions.

153.   Bampton fair. As early as the 13th century this little town on the river Batherm, just above its confluence with the Exe, had an annual October fair. Originally a great west-country sheep fair, it became famous country-wide for the sale of Exmoor ponies. Farmers, horse traders, gypsies and cheapjacks crowded into the town.

154. Bampton fair, *c*.1900. A shaggy-coated pony awaits his fate. The fall of the auctioneer's hammer may mean he is driven to the station and to fresh fields – or to a continental horse-meat abattoir.

155. Three-horse team delivering oil to a farm at Netherexe in 1912.

156. A four-horse team drags tree trunks across the heavy Devon clay on its way to the sawmills. Tiverton is internationally renowned for the manufacture of band-saws and sophisticated forestry machinery.

157.   Ploughing match at Cruwys Morchard in 1936. The Cruwys Morchard Ploughing Society still holds ploughing matches. Competitors come from all over the country to take part and there are also events for tractor-drawn ploughs.

158   Mayor's Sunday. By tradition, the mayor in his splendid robes of office, accompanied by the town clerk, councillors, beadle and mace-bearer, goes in procession to St Peter's church on the first Sunday after his election. Before mass-tailoring there were some 16 bespoke tailors in the town; here, master tailor Mayor Wakefield sets off in style.

159.   (*Above right*) Mayor's Sunday, 1903. Mayor Tom Lake, elected for a second time, decided to attend service not at St Peter's but at his own place of worship, the Congregational church. He proceeded there, accompanied by the usual escort, via Angel Hill.

160.   (*Right*) Mayor's Sunday, 1903. The deputy mayor, Alderman William Thorne, was outraged by this break with tradition. He refused to go with the mayor and was backed by the majority of the councillors. Defiantly, they made their way to St Peter's via Bampton and Newport Streets but, without an escort, their procession lacked authenticity.

161. Unknown soldiers. The Devons at Tiverton on parade on the brow of Angel Hill in October 1914. Angel Terrace above them is a steep rise, once known as the Ramparts (probably a strongpoint continuing the castle defences). Cellars and through-tunnels lie under the pathway. The handsome lamp standard replaced a former stone obelisk.

162. Tiverton artisans. Golf in Tiverton began seriously in 1932 when James Braid laid out the course at Post Hill. By 1936, a keen artisans section was enjoying the game, for a small subscription and subject to minor restrictions on the use of the clubhouse and hours of play, thanks largely to the encouragement of Sir John and Lady Amory, seen with them here at Knightshayes.

163. Knightshayes: a convalescent home for the United States Air Force sick and wounded in World War Two. Here, in the lengthening shadows, they are trying their skill on the putting green (now gone) which was reputed to be a fiendishly difficult, contoured one.

164. Joyce Wethered (Lady Amory, who married Sir John, 3rd Baronet, in 1937) here demonstrates to spectators, including Henry Cotton, Enid Wilson and Simone Lacoste, her famous free swing. She dominated golf in the 1920s, winning the English Ladies' Championship four times, the British Ladies' Open five times, and the Worplesdon Mixed Foursomes eight times between 1922 and 1936. The press callled her 'Queen of the Links' and Henry Cotton said she was 'Our answer to Bobby Jones'.

165. Tiverton's last horse-drawn fire engine. When the maroon sounded, the horses were unharnessed from the council refuse-carts by the workmen who galloped bareback to the fire station. Extra horses were sometimes hired from the *Angel* or *Palmerston*.

166. 'The Alderman Pinkstone', Tiverton's first motorised fire engine, beside St Peter's lych-gate in 1924. Chief Constable Mercer is in command, and the confident-looking dog, the team's mascot, seems to appreciate the importance of the occasion.

167. The Gospel Mission Van, a familiar sight up and down the valley before the war. Tiverton had many 'alternative' sects, most of them strongly evangelical, and a huge signboard, the length of a cottage in Barrington Street, demanded 'Where Will You Spend Eternity?'.

168. Tivertonians and Blundellians, near and far, love fun. The Rev. Richard Knight R.N. (with monkey), a popular day boy. In the 1930s, town boys were finally given their own house, 'Milestones'. He is seen here in Sydney, with H.M.S. *Implacable*. The message reads 'Look What Undernourishment has done for this poor man. Not even the Paybob can fatten him up. Give Generously. Food for Britain.'

169. Quinquennial service at St Peter's, still observed by Blundell's. Eton collars and strawyards have long been discontinued.

170. Queen Elizabeth's wedding veil, 1952. Heathcoat's, renowned for their 'up-market' net and lace, are making the bridal veil. In 1973 they made the veil for Princess Anne and in 1981 supplied silk veiling for Lady Diana Spencer on her marriage to H.R.H. the Prince of Wales.

171. America loved the Heathcoat nets. The wife of the Californian representative wrote in the *Heathcoat Chronicle* in April 1932: 'Heathcoat nets are used by every large studio in Hollywood ... pastel colours are most suitable ... the nets are principally used for dance dresses and evening gowns ... a telephone call for 500 yards would not be an unusual order'. When the Sadler's Wells ballet, with its prima ballerina Margot Fonteyn, visited the States, their tutus were all of Heathcoat net.

172. Visit of Sir Stafford Cripps, Minister of Aircraft Production, to the Heathcoat factory in 1945. During the war, the factory had produced parachutes and aircraft components.

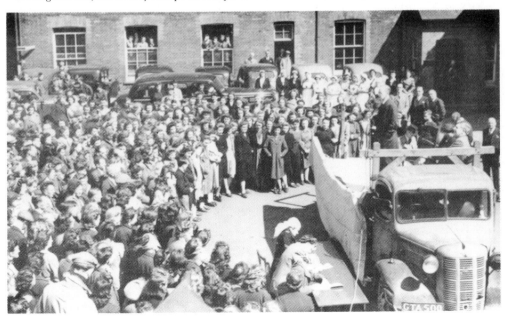

173. Sharland's Court, 1989. Much of old Tiverton (for example, the old posting hotel, *The Palmerston*) was bulldozed after the war. This timber-strapped passageway survives. It led from the serge-master's house (now the Lowman Restaurant) to a courtyard (now modernised), surrounded by his workers' cottages with their communal privy, here draped with ivy, and single common tap or pump. Tiverton was riddled with these picturesque courts, some dating back to the 16th century when a wool-making process, 'warping the chains', was carried out in them.

174. A Bridge Too Far? Twyford, the Town of the Two Fords, was unsure whether to welcome the new Link Road Bridge (1988) spanning the Exe to the north of the town. It carries traffic from Junction 27 of the M5 to the coastal towns of Bideford and Barnstaple. Here, in 1989, the functional bridge crosses the drought-stricken Exe as it struggles towards the sea.

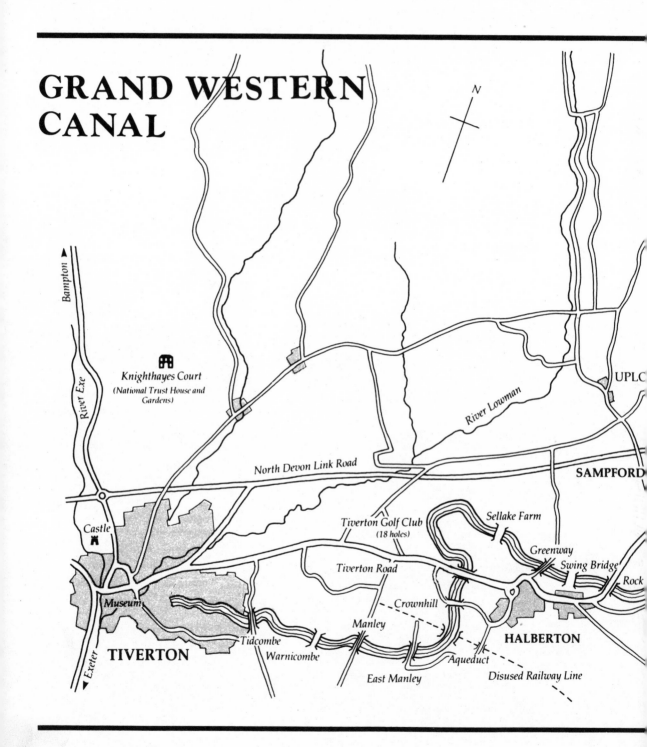

GRAND WESTERN CANAL